A Guide to Starting Psychotherapy Groups

A Guide to Starting Psychotherapy Groups

John R. Price
David R. Hescheles
A. Rae Price

Academic Press

San Diego   London   Boston   New York   Sydney   Tokyo   Toronto

Academic Press
A Division of Harcourt, Inc.
525 B Street, Suite 1900, San Diego, California 92101-4495, USA
http://www.apnet.com

Academic Press
24–28 Oval Road, London NW1 7DX
http://www.hbuk.co.uk/ap/

Library of Congress Catalog Card Number 99-63952
International Standard Book Number 0-12-564745-X

PRINTED IN THE UNITED STATES OF AMERICA
99 00 01 02 03 04 MM 9 8 7 6 5 4 3 2 1

Dedicated to
Murray and Smitty

CONTENTS

CONTRIBUTORS

ANNE ALONSO, Ph.D., Clinical Professor, Harvard Medical School, Massachusetts General Hospital Faculty, The Fielding Institute, Boston, Massachusetts

GARY M. BURLINGAME, Ph.D., Professor of Psychology, Brigham Young University, Provo, Utah

ADDIE FUHRIMAN, Ph.D., Assistant to President and Professor of Psychology, Brigham Young University, Provo, Utah

JOHN GLADFELTER, Ph.D., Faculty, The Fielding Institute, Dallas, Texas

DAVID R. HESCHELES, Psy.D., Private Practice, Oakdale, New York

LEON HOFFMAN, Ph.D., Independent Practice, Chicago, Illinois

JOHN J. O'HEARNE, M.D., Clinical Professor of Medicine, University of Missouri School of Medicine at Kansas City, Adjunct Professor of Sociology, University of Missouri at Kansas City, Kansas City, Missouri

A. RAE PRICE, Ph.D., Retired, Shawnee Mission, Kansas

JOHN R. PRICE, Ph.D., Private Practice, Kansas City, Missouri

ALBERT E. RIESTER, Ed.D., Professor, Trinity University, Clinical Professor, University of Texas Health Science Center; Psychologist, Southwest Mental Health Center, San Antonio, Texas

SHELDON D. ROSE, Ph.D., Professor, School of Social Work, University of Wisconsin, Madison, Wisconsin

J. SCOTT RUTAN, Ph.D., Senior Faculty, Boston Institute for Psychotherapy, Boston, Massachusetts

EMANUEL SHAPIRO, Ph.D., Senior Faculty, Group Therapy Department, Post Graduate Center for Mental Health, New York, New York

WALTER N. STONE, M.D., Professor, Department of Psychiatry, University of Cincinnati, Cincinnati, Ohio

PREFACE

A few years ago, at an annual meeting of the American Group Psychotherapy Association, David Hescheles and John Price were discussing their successes and failures in getting clients into groups. They also talked about their techniques for starting new groups. I think it was David who said: "We ought to write some of this down so others could profit from our experiences." Thus was born *A Guide to Starting Psychotherapy Groups*.

Group psychotherapy makes sense. Group psychotherapists can come from many professions: Psychology, psychiatry, social work, marriage and family counseling, nursing, educational counseling. ... At the present time, there is a paucity of trained group psychotherapists. (And how many human beings out there could profit from it—an impossible number to determine.) The purpose of this guide, then, is to encourage more therapists to get competent and thorough training and, subsequently, to begin serving some of their clientele by conducting groups.

This volume not only describes the process of starting groups; it also gives important information and suggestions from successful group therapists. Scattered throughout the text are vignettes from therapists' own group experiences. Also included is such information as how to keep track of referrals and group attendance, processes that can put off the would-be group therapist.

When you start your first group, you'll probably experience a number of benumbing thoughts and feelings, to wit, "What have I gotten myself into?"; "Will I be able to 'do' group psychotherapy?" and so on. This book will address issues and give you the information needed to quiet these fears. We want to give you the assurance needed to begin the process.

As you proceed, of course, your experiences, both clinical with your groups and professional through continuing education, will diminish doubt and increase feelings of competence.

One major concern has to do with how you market group therapy to your individual clients. We offer you some helpful answers to this question.

Another nagging doubt might be generating referrals elsewhere for your groups. Again, herein are some practical suggestions for this process. If you've considered the possibility of doing your group with another therapist, you'll find some useful help in the chapter on cotherapy.

I would underscore that this is a *guide* to starting groups, not an instructional treatise on how to do groups. (Much has been written about the processes of group therapy; there is pitifully little material on how to start groups.) Among the Appendixes is "Suggested Reading—a Beginning." These resources will point you to many other resources.

Also among the Appendixes is a short list of useful names and addresses. Our goal is to give you some helpful directions as you start on the path to becoming a group psychotherapist.

Chapters one through eight lead you from thinking about doing groups to your actually doing groups—after proper training, of course. The next chapters consider cotherapy and special groups, plus some helpful guidelines for group therapists. Then we've included an examination of the question "Does Group Psychotherapy Work?"—a question that is not easy to answer. Yet, as one group therapist writes in one of the vignettes, "If it works (even) in five out of ten cases, it works."

In chapters thirteen through seventeen, we've included articles on five different theoretical approaches to doing groups: Cognitive-Behavioral Group Psychotherapy, Psychodynamic Group Psychotherapy, Redecision Therapy, Transactional Analysis, and Psychoanalytic Group Psychotherapy. The process of doing groups, of course, is not limited to these five. Nor are these five mutually exclusive. These, at least, are among the more prominent theoretical approaches used in group therapy today. Your own training and experience may have emphasized one or more, but you will want at the outset to be acquainted with them all.

Finally, we have added something about terminations, both successful and unsuccessful, and about your role as the group therapist. While termination is hardly a part of starting groups, it is an important part of the whole therapeutic process—and one that can give the beginning group therapist some concern. Examining your role as a group therapist is, finally, the net thrown over the whole structure.

Included in the Appendixes, in addition to the list of suggested reading and the list of helpful names and addresses, are two more useful documents: "A Consumer's Guide to Group Psychotherapy," from the American Group Psychotherapy Association, and "An Introduction to Group Psychotherapy," which one author discusses with each candidate for therapy. In addition, he gives each potential client a copy. Finally, from *Psychotherapy Finances* we have included "A Glossary of Managed Care Terms." For further reference to the field of managed care, see Appendix E, "Suggested Reading—a Beginning."

A. Rae Price

ACKNOWLEDGMENTS

We have been fortunate to have Richard B. Cravens, Jacob Goering, and George McMichael read and give valuable suggestions to this manuscript. We are grateful to others who have assisted in the text's development: Harold Bernard, Bonnie Buchele, Mary Goulding, David Hawkins, John O'Hearne, and Barbara and Manny Shapiro. To Sandy Schuller and Sue Strong, we are grateful for assistance in the final preparation of the manuscript.

CHAPTER 1

Introduction and Definitions

JOHN R. PRICE, DAVID R. HESCHELES,
AND A. RAE PRICE

If you are a psychotherapist who works primarily with individual clients but who also wants to find out more about working with clients in groups, this book is for you. Our purpose is to help you become increasingly comfortable in starting your own groups.

You already know that individual psychotherapy can change lives for the better. Why, then, should you want to add a new modality, that of doing groups? The reasons are several:

- In many studies, group psychotherapy has been shown to be at least as effective—and in some studies even more effective—than individual psychotherapy.
- The cost to the client is considerably less.
- Your time is more efficiently used.
- Your income is increased.
- Managed care organizations are becoming increasingly aware of group psychotherapy's effectiveness.

Each of us, the two group psychotherapists who are the primary authors, has had over 20 years experience in working with groups. We know that groups work. And we know that leading psychotherapy groups is a skill that can be learned. (For a thorough look at the question "Does Group Psychotherapy Work?" see chapter XII.)

We also have had many discussions with skilled individual therapists who are uncomfortable in starting groups. Or they may have tried starting a group and found they did not have the techniques to get the group organized and moving. We offer you herein some useful ways to overcome both your reticence in starting groups and your fears about keeping them going.

Keep in mind as you use this guide that it is a *primer.* Its purpose is to assist you in *starting* groups, not in doing groups. You will want to familiarize yourself with the literature on doing groups—with the theory and practice as recorded by other experienced group psychotherapists. To help you begin this process, we have included a short list, "Suggested Reading—A Beginning," in Appendix E.

However, more important than familiarizing yourself with the literature on doing groups is considering your own training as a *group* psychotherapist, not only before and during your early stages as a group therapist but also as you continue to expand your group practice.

MacKenzie (1995), former president of the American Group Psychotherapy Association, addresses this issue:

> Some therapists who have been primarily trained in individual therapy can make the transition to the group situation smoothly. However, most experience some difficulty. The most common error is to move without conscious effort into treating individual patients in a group context. This may not be actively harmful, although it can demoralize the group and lead to premature dropouts. At the very least, such an error fails to capitalize on the energy of the group.... This results in less effective treatment. Group therapy, like individual therapy, can be harmful. This usually involves mishandling of affectively laden material. For example, disclosure of powerful personal material that receives no validation or response can be quite devastating. Anger, particularly anger in which the therapist directly or indirectly colludes, can create a scapegoating pattern that is particularly damaging. Issues surrounding subgrouping between members can also be hazardous. In short, group management skills are important when treating a group population that is by definition experiencing psychological difficulties (p. 20).

As part of your training, the American Group Psychotherapy Association (AGPA) recommends that you participate in a psychotherapy group a minimum of 60 hours. Irvin D. Yalom, in his seminal book *The Theory and Practice of Group Psychotherapy* (1995), summarizes reasons for your participation in a group before undertaking group leadership on your own; his words also underscore the powerful experiences that come from group interactions:

> A personal group experience has become widely accepted as an integral part of a training program. Such an experience may offer many types of learning not available elsewhere. You are able to learn at an emotional level what you may previously

have known only intellectually. You experience the power of the group—power to wound and to heal. You learn how important it is to be accepted by the group; what self-disclosure really entails; how difficult it is to reveal your secret world, your fantasies, feelings of vulnerability, hostility, and tenderness. You learn to appreciate your own strengths as well as weaknesses. You learn about your own preferred role in the group. Perhaps most striking of all, you learn about the role of the leader by becoming aware of your own dependency and your unrealistic appraisal of the leader's power and knowledge (Yalom, 1995, pp. 518–519).

In addition to your training through participating in a psychotherapy group, we encourage you to join, if you have not already done so, your local professional organizations. There you can take advantage in your own area of additional training sessions on working with clients in groups. Professionals in your area will be able to help you identify these organizations.

You will certainly want to consider joining the American Group Psychotherapy Association. Within AGPA are 32 local or regional affiliate societies. According to AGPA:

Special interests may be pursued through national, regional, and local committees; task forces and special interest groups involved with education, training, clinical practice, ethical standards, public policy, and research of group therapy theory and techniques.

AGPA membership is open to clinically trained professionals, researchers, students and trainees. The annual meeting of AGPA is held each February in various locales across the country. Membership in AGPA is not a prerequisite for attendance at the annual meeting.

At the annual meeting, you can select from a variety of sessions in the Institute and/or the Conference itself. The Conference bulletin for 1998 annual meeting explains the Institute as:

primarily designed for clinical professionals who meet the minimum requirements of a master's degree in a mental health profession including at least 100 hours of clinical psychotherapy experience. *Certain designated sections of the Institute are available to psychiatric residents, graduate students in mental health degree programs and mental health workers who work in a range of human service settings* (emphasis added).

During the Conference, half-day and full-day workshops are scheduled, plus lectures by nationally known group psychotherapists. Offered at the Conference, and of particular interest to any clinician wishing to begin the process of being certified as a group psychotherapist, is the Certificate Program #1. This program, under the direction of the National Registry of Certified Group Psychotherapists (NRCGP), is designed to:

provide a basic understanding of the theory, principles and application of group psychotherapy. This 12-hour didactic and discussion presentation (covers) group process and dynamics, types of group psychotherapies, clinical and ethical issues, group psychotherapy research and the history of group psychotherapy. At the con-

clusion of this program participants who attend all four sessions will be awarded a
certificate designating successful completion.

This program meets the 12-hour course requirement for the National Registry
of Certified Group Psychotherapists.

Further requirements for becoming a Certified Group Psychotherapist
(CGP), as listed in the National Registry of Certified Group Psychotherapists,
include 300 hours of group psychotherapy experience as a leader or coleader,
75 hours of group psychotherapy supervision, plus completed reference forms.

With the requisite clinical credential documentation, this certification can
apply to the following professions: psychiatry, psychology, social work, nursing, marriage and family therapy, clinical mental health counseling, and pastoral counseling.

For more information about AGPA, NRCGP, and for a membership application in AGPA, see "Helpful Names and Addresses" in Appendix A.

For psychologists, a valuable resource is Division 49, Group Psychology
and Group Psychotherapy, of the American Psychological Association (APA).
For further information, see "Helpful Names and Addresses" in Appendix A.

Another valuable resource for you, depending on where you are in your
career, is the Fielding Institute. The Institute is a regionally accredited graduate school offering degree programs in:

- Clinical Psychology (Ph.D.)
- Human & Organization Development (Ph.D., Ed.D.)
- Educational Leadership & Change (Ed.D.)
- Organizational Design & Effectiveness (M.A)

The Institute was founded in 1974

> on the principles of adult learning. Its scholar-practitioner model is designed to
> serve midcareer professionals who must maintain multiple commitments to family,
> work and community while earning an advanced degree. A networked learning
> community is formed from dynamic, scholarly and intellectual interactions by
> means of electronic communications combined with periodic face-to-face events at
> various locations.

For more information about the Fielding Institute, see "Helpful Names and
Addresses," Appendix A.

Remember that, although you may be apprehensive in starting your first
group, we are convinced that, with the guidance available to you, you will find
the professional experience rewarding for both you and your clients.

As you, no doubt, also know, approaches to treatment differ among group
psychotherapists. Table I and the following paragraphs briefly compare three
major theoretical orientations common to psychotherapists: time-limited,
Cognitive/Behavioral Focal groups; Psychodynamic groups; and Eclectic

TABLE I   A Comparison of Three Differing Theoretical Orientations to Group Psychotherapy

Functions	Time-limited Cognitive Behavior Focal	Psychodynamic	Eclectic, including Gestalt, Existential, Redecision Therapy, and others
Structure:	High structure	Low structure	Low to medium structure
Leadership:	Therapist's role as leader: strong	Leadership style: group directed	Leadership styles: vary
Goal orientation:	Highly goal oriented	General goals with emphasis on characterological changes	Moves toward defining specific goals
Emphasis:	Highly educational	Emphasis on insight	Emphasis on change in addition to understanding
Attention to:	Little attention to transference and psychodynamic issues	High attention to transference and psychodynamic issues	Attention to transference and other psychodynamic issues varies
Techniques:	Identifying unproductive thought patterns	Interpretation	Support
	Homework assignments to ameliorate thoughts and behaviors	Transference	Positive feedback
	Monitoring observable evidence for change	Interaction	Understanding payoffs for dysfunctional behavior
	Cognitive rehearsal role playing	Feedback	Learning more appropriate payoffs
	Desensitization	Analyzing resistance	
	Assertiveness training	Countertransference	
Entry/Exit:	Client commits for length of stay	Ongoing group; flexible entry and exit; emphasis on group preparation for new members	Ongoing group; flexible entry and exit

groups, including Gestalt Therapy, Existential Therapy, Redecision Therapy, Transactional Analysis, or a combination of these and other theoretical orientations. You may wish to earmark this table as you move through this volume, adding notes according to your own theoretical orientation.

No matter what your own theoretical orientation is, you will want to familiarize yourself with the other models. Therefore, we have included in the final chapters some introductory material on each of them: Cognitive Behavioral, Psychodynamic, Psychoanalytic, and Eclectic. "Eclectic," of course, as the word indicates, employs a variety of theoretical approaches. Under "Eclectic," we have selected only two approaches, Redecision Therapy and Transactional Analysis, although many others could be a part of this volume. (see "Suggested Reading—A Beginning," Appendix E.)

COGNITIVE BEHAVIORAL FOCAL GROUPS

The term "focal group" is well chosen: no matter for what problem the group is drawn together—alcohol abuse, uncontrolled anger, poor social skills—the group's focus is on changing the maladaptive behavior. Focal groups are common not only in institutions but also in out-patient settings.

Cognitive Behavioral Focal group therapists are not concerned with the why of behavior but with the spontaneous thought patterns of the person. Focal group therapists will identify unproductive thought patterns and work to change inappropriate behavior. To ameliorate the thoughts and, therefore, the behaviors, they will use various techniques: assigning homework, monitoring observable evidence for change, directing cognitive rehearsal role playing, using desensitization, and employing assertiveness training. The group is used to reinforce the leader's implementation of the structured program.

PSYCHODYNAMIC GROUPS

Although the term "Psychodynamic Group Psychotherapy" (the why of behavior) can encompass diverse approaches, three elements are necessary. The first of these deals with the group participants' intrapsychic life—their internal emotional life. That internal emotional life is made up of the clients' character structure, psychological defense patterns, problem solving techniques, internal conflicts, dependency issues, and their internal object relations—that is, relationships in the past which still influence or control their ways of relating to others and to themselves in the present.

The second of these deals with interpersonal style. The group closely observes exchanges in the here and now, recognizing that internalized conflicts are often played out in the present.

The third deals with the broad context within which the group is operating. This analysis takes into account the social structure of the group: the group's rules, the relationship of the individual to the group as well as the relationship of the group to the leader, and the way the group handles change. It also means examining the roles individuals play in the group, the norms for functioning in the group, and the limits and criteria for membership and inclusion in the group.

ECLECTIC GROUPS

Eclectic therapists integrate many themes into a blend that works well for them. For example, they might use a Gestalt two-chair exercise to help a client resolve an internal conflict with another person. They might use their own feelings about the client as a way of understanding the client, thus employing countertransference as a tool. By emphasizing the client's taking responsibility for his or her own feelings and behavior, they would use a concept stressed in Redecision Therapy. In analyzing payoffs for dysfunctional behavior and replacing with healthier, more functional payoffs, they would be using Reinforcement Theory.

In using Transactional Analysis, the therapist, using ego states (the Parent, Adult, and Child), describes the transactions between group members to identify how they are relating to each other. This could further lead to an examination of how the group members relate to family members, thus highlighting the problems which brought them to therapy initially.

REFERENCES

Fuhriman, A., & Burlingame, G. (1994). Does group psychotherapy work? *Handbook of group psychotherapy: An empirical and clinical synthesis* (pp. 7–20). New York: John Wiley & Sons.

MacKenzie, K. R. (1995). Rationale for group psychotherapy in managed care. In K. R. MacKenzie (Ed.), *Effective use of group therapy in managed care*. Washington, DC: American Psychiatric Press.

Yalom, I. D. (1995). *The theory and practice of group psychotherapy* (4th ed.). New York: Basic Books.

Attitudes and Expectations

JOHN R. PRICE AND A. RAE PRICE

One time, I had in a group a Catholic priest, a Lutheran
minister, and an Episcopalian priest. The day one of them got
mad at one of the others and fervently told him to "go to hell,"
I knew we were going to have a good group.

No matter what your theoretical orientation is—and successful group psychotherapists come in all shapes and sizes of theoretical orientations—a common base exists for building successful groups. As a group psychotherapist, you will find that your clients will significantly profit—intrapsychically, interpersonally, and behaviorally—from this powerful treatment modality. Your attitude and expectations concerning group psychotherapy, as well as those of your client, are as important as the theoretical orientation you bring or the apprehension your client brings.

Let's look first at your clients' probable mind-set. Uncommon are the clients who enter the psychotherapist's office either wanting or expecting treatment to take place in a group setting. In spite of their having spent a great deal of time among clusters of people—families, colleagues, neighbors, fellow students, parishioners—they are often uncomfortable discussing their emotional pain with others.

What about the mind-set of you, the therapist? The experienced group psychotherapist, unlike his or her clients, knows well the efficacy of groups. Rather than thinking "Is this a client who could benefit from a group?", the group psychotherapist is more apt to think "Is there any reason this client should *not* be in a therapy group?"

Fundamental to the process of working with your client, therefore, is your examining your own basic approach. The search for reasons the client would *not* profit from a psychotherapy group directs not only your thinking but also the manner in which you market the idea of group psychotherapy to clients. Your attitude and expectations and those of your client differ; the client's apprehension must be assuaged by your confidence.

CHAPTER 3

Referrals to Group

JOHN R. PRICE AND A. RAE PRICE

It was the first session of a long-term psychodynamic group. Nine members made a 20-session initial commitment to group as part of the contract. About 30 minutes into the session, a male member announced that he would have to miss the next six sessions because his soccer league had changed to the night of the group.

To my surprise, the members of the group challenged him on commitment; they asked if he had made the same 20-session commitment that they had made. They asked what was more important, soccer or the group. He was quite defensive and rationalized his announcement throughout the process.

With 10 minutes left, I told him it was a difficult decision he had to make, but I hoped he would come back as I could see how invigorating he would be for the group. He said, "You mean, if I choose to miss the six sessions, I can't come back?" I said that we were out of time but we could discuss it further next week. He protested that he would have to miss a game if he came next week. I empathized with him and said, "I know it is hard to be in two places at the same time." He came back the next week and remained for the following sessions.

Your clients for group, as with many group psychotherapists, will come primarily from your client base. However, you may also want or need to market yourself as a group therapist to colleagues and the public in general. As you establish a firm reputation for leading psychotherapy groups, you will get direct referrals to your groups. However, in order to build this reputation, you must often take other actions.

One of the most common and widely accepted methods for getting the word out is to send announcements to a wide variety of colleagues: social workers, psychologists, psychiatrists and other physicians, counselors in education, and pastoral counselors. Send flyers to social service and welfare organizations, a list of which you can find in your local yellow pages. Appear as often as possible on community forums and lecture platforms, where you can underscore your group psychotherapy interest.

Explore connections with Health Maintenance Organizations (HMO's) and Preferred Provider Organizations (PPO's). In order to get on provider panels, call the Provider Relations Office of the insurance company in question to obtain an application.

For therapists who are already providers, call the insurance companies regarding coverage for group psychotherapy. Most insurance companies provide the same coverage for group psychotherapy as for individual therapy. They will give the allowable number of visits per year for your clients, depending on their mental health benefits. Some plans have a dollar maximum per year which, of course, is better for group psychotherapy. For a helpful glossary of acronyms and managed care terms, see Appendix D.

Contact Motivational and Self-Improvement Training Groups, again through a listing in the yellow pages. Offer to work with alcohol and drug treatment centers.

Find out about local self-help groups and ask to speak at their meetings; your local Mental Health Association, as well as some of your local churches and synagogues, may publish or at least know of a directory of self-help groups. Talk with professionals in child protective services offices and in local probation departments if you are starting a group for children and adolescents. Work with your senior services centers if you are starting a group for older people and/or retirees.

Go to the source, recommends consultant Nichols (1995) in a helpful resource for behavioral health providers, *Psychotherapy Finances*. (See "Helpful Names and Addresses," Appendix A.):

> For example, if you're running a men's anger management group, you could go to your *local probation department,* department of human services, and child protective services office. For a women's support group, you might want to try these options:
>
> 1. put a notice (professional announcement) in local publications and therapeutic newsletters;
> 2. place pamphlets in bookstores, church foyers, community center, all with permission, of course;
> 3. go on a local radio talk show;
> 4. visit area ob/gyns. Visits to local pediatricians would be appropriate for children's groups on self-esteem and coping skills.

Some therapists are more comfortable being assertive than are others; you must select your own degree of assertiveness.

Cross (1995) states that

> Whether the aim is to establish a comprehensive group psychotherapy program within a clinic or group practice setting or to market a more limited program to managed care companies developed by an individual or small group of practition-

ers, the primary goal is the same: to deliver clinically needed and relevant group psychotherapy in a cost-effective manner to patients who will most benefit from this therapeutic intervention, either as the only treatment modality or in conjunction with individual treatment.

Johnson and Riester (1998) describe an activity group therapy program which has been operating for five years at the Southwest Mental Health Center in San Antonio:

> In a residential treatment center, developing such a program requires ongoing communication with administrators, supervisory staff, and clinicians. In a residential setting there are formal supervisory structures for nursing services, special education, therapeutic recreation and the clinicians. Although the clinician who developed the group program was a senior staff member in the organization, the success of a group service requires ongoing support of all subgroups in the system.

> The first step in launching the activity group program in the residential center requires the submission of a written plan specifying the goals, meeting times, staffing requirements, and how and when supervision will be provided. After approval at the Program Director and CEO levels of the governance structure, the group leader must maintain ongoing communication with the supervisors on the shift when the groups are being conducted.

> When interacting with the staff, the group therapists gained credibility because they valued the input of the mental health workers. Their suggestions were used to improve behavior management during the group sessions. Also, the group leaders recognized the emotional and physical demands in working with severely disturbed children for a full eight-hour shift. This validation of their "front line" role prevented the group therapists from assuming the role of expert in the communication process. In brief, the group leaders validated the dedication, skill, patience, and hard work of the staff who interacted with severely emotionally disturbed children and adolescents on a full time basis. A collaborative spirit was created between staff and group therapists as they exchanged information to improve the quality of patient care in the facility.

> The following program elements were identified as central to the success in establishing groups in a residential treatment center for severely emotionally disturbed adolescents and children:

> 1. Full administrative approval at all levels of the governance structure must be obtained.

> 2. The activities, intervention approaches and goals were congruent with the age and developmental levels of the clients.

> 3. The group schedule was established so it would not compete with other therapeutic and special educational services on the campus

> 4. The group sessions were perceived as positive and the clients looked forward to the group meetings with leaders who had a caring and empathic attitude.

> 5. Ongoing supervision was provided for the coleaders who conducted the groups to deal with a range of countertransference issues and planning details.

> 6. The mental health workers had the opportunity to participate in the process and knew the main purpose of the group experiences and activities.

> In summary, approximately 52 adolescents and children are receiving group therapy at the Southwest Mental Health Center. On an annual basis, a presentation is made to the Board of Directors of the Center to highlight the purpose, scope, and

outcomes of the group program. The program elements that were followed are examples of group communication skills that are applicable to both the larger organization and within the therapeutic groups.

REFERENCES

Cross, C. D. (1995). Organizing group psychotherapy programming in managed care settings. In K. R. MacKenzie (Ed.), *Effective use of group therapy in managed care* (p. 32). Washington, DC: American Psychiatric Press.

Johnson, C., & Riester, A. (1998). Group activities for children and adolescents: An activity group therapy approach. *Journal of Child and Adolescent Group Therapy, 8, 2,* 78–88.

MacKenzie, K. R. (1995). Rationale for group psychotherapy in managed care. In K. R. MacKenzie (Ed.), *Effective use of group therapy in managed care* (p. 20). Washington, DC: American Psychiatric Press.

Nichols, Marjorie (1995, June). Marketing therapy groups. *Psychotherapy Finances, 21,* 6.

CHAPTER 4

Selecting Clients for Group Psychotherapy

JOHN R. PRICE, DAVID R. HESCHELES,
AND A. RAE PRICE

In one group, one of the women was very calm, not participating in the group discussion about fear of me, about my mystery, and their fascination of the mystery which they attributed to me. They saw me as both mysterious and powerful. We were doing an analysis of transference. "You don't seem to be involved in this," I said to the woman. "Are you?" She said "No, I'm not." "How do you manage that?" I asked. She replied: "I just imagine you sitting on the toilet." The whole group roared. That was either the end of the analysis of transference—or just the beginning.

As stated earlier, the group psychotherapist is apt to ask "Is there any reason this client should *not* be in a therapy group?" Yalom (1995) suggests that the way to select clients is to exclude all those who cannot work in group and then accept all others.

However, suitability for group psychotherapy does not necessarily indicate a client's readiness for group. Assessing a client's readiness will be dealt with shortly. First, let's look at the those clients for whom group therapy would *not* be advisable.

CRITERIA FOR EXCLUSION

Yalom identified as poor candidates those who are:

- Brain damaged
- Paranoid
- Hypochondriacal

- Addicted to drugs or alcohol
- Acutely psychotic
- Sociopathic

Although it can be argued that, under controlled situations, almost all of these potential clients could benefit from a Focal Group experience, they are generally poor candidates for most groups. On the other hand, as you gain experience, you may find that clients who are paranoid or hypochondriacal *may* be candidates for a psychotherapy group on a selective basis. Also, those who are actively utilizing drugs and/or abusing alcohol, may, with additional aid from support groups such as Alcoholics and/or Narcotics Anonymous, be good candidates for group.

In addition, the following could be added to the list of poor candidates for group:

1. Clients whose characterological defenses are so strong that they are unmotivated to learn about themselves or improve their skills
2. Clients who cannot or will not control physical violence
3. Clients who will not accept or agree to the initial contract.

What are some of the factors in assessing a client's readiness for entry into a group? That readiness must be assessed both in terms of the client's recognition and in terms of your seeing that the client can evolve as a group member.

SELECTING CLIENTS FOR COGNITIVE BEHAVIORAL FOCAL GROUPS

Obviously, psychotherapists leading Focal groups generally have less choice in the selection of clients than do therapists leading the other two theoretical orientations: Focal group psychotherapists are dealing with clients who are concentrating on a specific symptom, for example, shyness or agoraphobia, whereas the Psychodynamic and the Eclectic groups will not be so constructed.

Those clients who are candidates for Focal groups must exhibit some or all of the characteristics for which the group is being formed. For example, a candidate for an agoraphobia focal group might be selected for one or more of the following reasons:

1. The client has anxiety about being in a place or situation.
2. The client must have an escape route before he will be in a specific place.
3. The client will not travel alone outside his home.

Focal group leaders usually rule out personality disorders such as borderline and narcissistic. Additionally, they will usually rule out severely depressed individuals—except in institutional settings where such individuals may be appropriately treated within a group. Finally, those who are selected for a Focal group must be willing to make the commitment for the entire number of sessions.

SELECTING CLIENTS FOR PSYCHODYNAMIC AND ECLECTIC GROUPS

As you consider clients for group, remember that you are assessing your clients' *potentials* to profit from the group experience. As the group develops, your clients' introspective and empathetic skills will develop. Clients will recognize different feelings, needs, and wishes of other group members, and will be able to establish, either verbally and/or nonverbally, an understanding of the pain of others.

Therefore, at the outset, you must differentiate between your client's demonstrating a fitness and readiness for group and your recognition of the client's *potential* for helping her- or himself and others grow through the group experience.

Your clients demonstrate that they are fit and are ready for the group when:

1. they clearly recognize their emotional pain
2. they recognize that at least some of their problems are interpersonal
3. they hope that they may achieve results from group psychotherapy.

You assess the client as being ready for group when the client, in your judgment, has the *potential*:

1. to tolerate anxiety generated by the group experience, such as giving and getting feedback or revealing emotions and struggles in a group setting
2. to be influenced by others: listening to what others are saying, considering a suggested change in interpersonal style;
3. to empathize and identify with others; putting themselves at least temporarily in the shoes of another person; seeing others as separate with different feelings, needs, and wishes;
4. to learn to be helpful to others; suggesting changes which the client, the sender, believes will be useful;
5. in later development, to give what is helpful, emotionally and behaviorally, to another person in the group.

As the group develops cohesion—a sense of "groupness"—with the enveloping sense of trust and emotional safety, individual clients are simultaneously developing their ability to be helpful to others. At the outset, however, in selecting clients for group psychotherapy, you need only to ask yourself the basic question "Is there any reason this client *shouldn't* be in a group," using the above guidelines to help you answer the question.

SOME SPECIAL CONSIDERATIONS FOR PSYCHODYNAMIC GROUPS

In starting a new Psychodynamic group or replacing graduates or terminees in an ongoing group, MacKenzie and Livesley(1983) points out that you will enhance the chances for a successful group by conceptualizing four social roles that are frequently found in groups: (1) the social–emotional role; (2) the task-oriented or structuring role; (3) the individualistic or cautionary role; and (4) the defiant role.

1. The social–emotional role: This role is played by clients who establish relationships easily. These clients are often caretakers who facilitate group cohesion, trust, and interpersonal engagement. Their ability to trust allows them to self-disclose early and sets a model for others. They often bring out isolated members and make genuine emotional contact with them.

Even though these individuals are crucial to the group's life, particularly in the early stages, they can be a liability because they impede confrontation and challenge. The pathology of the individuals may lead to assuming this role. They often trust too much; they can be excessively needy and dependent on others. Their need to be accepted often leads to difficulties in their asserting their opinions and sticking up for themselves. Their self-disclosure is often superficial because it lacks exploring negative aspects of their emotional conflicts.

2. The task-oriented or structuring role: As if in a management position, these clients keep the goal of the group in mind. If the group strays, they will point it out. Although their behavior may often seem controlling, their concern is usually not with power but with adherence to the rules. In the beginning stages of the group, their value lies in reducing ambiguity by helping establish explicit goals and norms. Their contributions help reduce anxiety, thereby reducing group anxiety. Their concern with results also makes them useful in transferring in-group learning to outside situations.

These task-oriented clients, however, often may have significant relationship problems. They find it difficult to empathize in an affective way and often do not seem to comprehend other group members' feelings. They often compensate for this lack of comprehension by giving too much analysis and advice for concrete problem-solving. This can drive others away. Their own avoidance of emotions, because it lacks structure, leads to a stilted, formalistic way of relating. They dampen spontaneity and have difficulty having fun and enjoying things.

3. The individual or cautionary role: These clients stress the importance of personal responsibility and champion the cause of autonomy at all costs. Although they are often skeptical about the benefits of the group and are reluctant to participate or reveal much about themselves, their value to the group's development is their emphasis on self-direction. They foster awareness of the dangers of total reliance on someone else for a sense of well-being. These members are often at risk for premature termination and can disrupt the cohesiveness of the group through their own noninvolvements. The pathology for these clients is their excessive need for autonomy, which often leaves them socially isolated and frustrates others' concerns for them. If they have intimate relationships, these are often fraught with anger and distrust.

4. The defiant role: These clients' interpersonal stances are combative. They are familiar with, often even comfortable with, being angry and accepting the hostility of others. They are often a contradiction, in that they can be insensitive to nuances, yet be uncanny in their ability to pinpoint vulnerable areas of other group members' emotional functioning.

The group is often ambivalent toward these members, seeing them as important, yet wanting to eject them in order to maintain cohesion and safety.

However, the defiant group members can be extremely important to the group because they can force the group members to deal with conflict and conflict resolution. They force new behaviors from the "nice" members; these "nice" members may have learned to tolerate anger but are now learning to perceive confrontation as a vehicle toward emotional growth. They are particularly challenging when the group is avoiding important psychological work.

Pathologically, these members often have great difficulty in intimate relationships. They are often rejected and, at times, can have an identity confusion. They often elicit such anger from the group that the anger becomes self-destructive for the client.

During the early stages of a group, role behaviors usually occur in stereotypical fashion. While each of the four roles is important for the group to progress, each role obviously has negative implications for the individual filling that role. It may seem, at the beginning of a group, there is only one individual per role. However, if the group is to progress, the limited size of the group requires individuals to learn different roles. This means that each must modify rigid, interpersonal patterns and learn greater flexibility in functioning.

REFERENCE

Mackenzie, K., & Livesley, W. (1983). A developmental model for brief group therapy. In R. Dies & K. Mackenzie (Eds.) *Advances in Group Psychotherapy.* New York: International Universities Press, Inc.

CHAPTER 5

Orienting and Educating Clients*

JOHN R. PRICE AND DAVID R. HESCHELES

This one comes under the heading "You Can Work with Anything that Happens." I had a fairly new group. It was summertime, in the 1970s. A single, rather lonely guy in his 20s had just returned from a three-day weekend at Esalen. Monday night he came to group. Suddenly, in the midst of us, he began taking off his clothes. Soon, he was stark naked. At Esalen over the weekend, everybody had taken their clothes off. So he brought it back to group.

Some group members were laughing, some were upset. One woman, who thought she was really sexually liberated, yelled "Put your clothes back on."

We talked about the group members' reactions, and she, the "sexually liberated woman," began to talk about and work on her strict upbringing, realizing she was not as free as she thought she was.

In group, you can work with anything that happens.

ORIENTING AND EDUCATING CLIENTS FOR COGNITIVE BEHAVIORAL FOCAL GROUPS

Cognitive Behavioral Focal groups often start with only bare bones client orientation. These groups are directly goal-oriented; clients entering the group can acknowledge that goal—for example, overcoming shyness or stopping the abuse of alcohol. Because these are homogeneous groups and because client selection is predetermined and focused, these groups generally cohere readily. They have a sense of purpose and a time frame in which to accomplish that purpose. Thus, the pregroup orientation and education factors diminish in importance.

---

* A portion of this work reprinted with permission from Johnson, C. & Riester, A. (1998). Group activities for children and adolescents: an activity group therapy approach. *Journal of Child and Adolescent Group Therapy*, 2, 78–88.

ORIENTING AND EDUCATING CLIENTS FOR PSYCHODYNAMIC AND ECLECTIC GROUPS

Bearing in mind that the new referral may, at first, be unreceptive to the idea of group therapy, orientation towards acceptance must come slowly.

The following steps can be among those to assist you in gaining the client's acceptance.

1. Introducing the idea of group therapy: The first step with a relatively new client is to casually mention that you do—or are thinking of doing—group therapy. For example, if you already have a therapy group, a casual remark when bringing a new client into the office can be "Have a seat anywhere you're comfortable. As you can see from the number of chairs available, I do group therapy."

2. Or, if you are just starting a group, you can introduce yourself to a new client by saying, "I am _____ _____; I do individual and group therapy." These kinds of casual statements can constitute the first mention of group psychotherapy. They may scarcely be heard, but they can introduce the idea.

Given the client's readiness, you can now decide when to mention group psychotherapy specifically for his or her treatment. The goal is both to establish rapport with the client and to reduce the client's anxiety about group therapy. For general referrals who have not been referred specifically for group psychotherapy, this process could take three to six sessions. For the client who has been specifically referred, an interview or two may be all that is needed.

The specific mention of group therapy, then, as part of the treatment plan will not only vary in time but also in approach. For example, the client may speak of his or her poor interpersonal relationships: shyness or abrasive behavior in groups, difficulties in marriage, childrearing frustrations, or job dissatisfaction. As the client dwells on his or her poor interpersonal relationships, you can then mention, "We might want to think about the possibility of *group* psychotherapy to help with that." Or when the client talks about difficulties in expressing feelings in intimate relationships, you can say, "That is an area that can perhaps be successfully developed in a group setting."

The specific mention, then, follows as a result of the therapist and the client's identifying a problem: poor interpersonal relations, difficulty in expressing feelings, or discomfort in other areas.

The specific mention of group psychotherapy can, and perhaps should, occur at the very end of a session. When the client responds with a question "What is group psychotherapy?", you can then reply "We're out of time in this session. Let's talk more about this next time." Remember that clients often have a built-in apprehension about revealing themselves in front of others. Therefore, referring to the possibility of group therapy at the end of a session allows the client the opportunity to ponder the suggestion before your next session.

You had previously mentioned to the client that you do group psychotherapy when the client noticed the number of chairs in the office or when you introduced yourself as a group as well as an individual psychotherapist. You had planted the idea with the client. The next step is to more formally discuss group psychotherapy with the client. Having set the stage by mentioning group psychotherapy both generally and specifically, you are prepared to go into more detail regarding what group psychotherapy is all about. In the interest of successfully marketing group psychotherapy to the client, keep in mind that the more information the client has about the process, the lower her or his anxiety will be.

You might elect not to discuss group therapy with a client in the session immediately after your first suggesting it. However, you will want to go back and remind the client that you had mentioned group psychotherapy. In discussing the group psychotherapy process, tell the potential group member that you have three specific areas you want to address:

1. The contract with each client, made up of five ground rules by which clients are to abide. Tell them: "I will give you a copy of these ground rules before the session is over today."
2. Some administrative details about a therapy group
3. Your style as a group psychotherapist.

Incidentally, this recitation usually takes only about 5 minutes.

At the end of the enumeration of specifics, give the client the copy of what you've just described, "An Introduction to Group Psychotherapy." (See Appendix B.) Then ask the client if he or she has any questions; if so, discuss the these questions at this point.

If there are no questions, you can say: "You might want to think about this, and we can discuss it further in a subsequent session." Some clients respond by saying immediately that they are ready to go into a group. Although this is not a rarity, more often clients need a period of time to think about the process of group therapy as another necessary step in their progress. Should a client respond after the discussion of group with "I'll try," you should tell her or him that she is not going to experience the full impact of group therapy in less than 4 to 6 months. Hence, you will ask for an oral contract to stay in group for at least 4 months. You may add that you have found this to be the minimum amount of time necessary for clients to begin to benefit from the group experience.

After the discussion of group therapy, should a client respond with a refusal, bear in mind that the reasons for the refusal are almost invariably parallel to or a part of what brought the client to therapy in the first place. In the event of a refusal, explore this parallel with the client. Following are some hypothetical examples:

Reasons for Refusal	*Reasons for Group*
"I am a private person."	Being an isolate, a private person, is what brought the client to the therapist. Group is the tool of choice to use in overcoming the problem.
"If the therapist has to have a 'no sex' rule, the people must be sexually dangerous."	Group can be a safe place in which to learn intimacy and overcome jealousy.
"Why the 'no physical violence'?"	Group can help the client be more accepting of his anger and learn how to deal with it more appropriately.

Another approach to introducing the client to group therapy is contained in the following article by Leon Hoffman, "Preparing the Client for Group Psychotherapy."

CHAPTER 6

Preparing the Patient for Group Psychotherapy*

LEON HOFFMAN

The purpose of this interview is to review the necessary and salient issues for an adult patient's entry into an open, outpatient psychotherapy group. What follows is an unedited, transcribed interview, the result of an unrehearsed, spontaneous conversation elucidating those elements essential for a patient to know and agree to before entering such a group. Complete historical data have been obtained during earlier sessions with the patient and are assumed here (see addendum). An actor plays the role of the prospective patient. Psychotherapists conducting groups using different approaches or in different settings may choose to modify selected aspects accordingly to best suit their group needs.

INTERVIEW

Dr. Hi, Mary, how are you?
Pt. Hello, Dr. Hoffman. I'm fine, thanks. How are you?

*Reprinted with permission from Hoffman, L. (1998). Preparing the patient for group psychotherapy. *The Group Psychologist*, 8(2), 4–14.

Dr. Great. So much has been going on these last few weeks, especially with planning for the best timing for you to join the therapy group we've been talking about, which group, and exactly when you might enter it.

Pt. Do you think we'll do that soon?

Dr. Do you mean actually going in and starting group?

Pt. Right.

Dr. I think we could even start in the next week or two, although there should never be an urgency about group psychotherapy, since it's never an emergency room treatment. But you and I have been meeting originally twice a week and once a week for 45 minutes during the past 10 months. And more recently we've been talking about how working in the psychotherapy group would augment and develop much that you've been focusing on in individual therapy. The kind of therapy we were talking about is sometimes referred to as "combined therapy," which refers to the same therapist's conducting both the individual and the group psychotherapy, and is what we'd be doing here. So, in combined therapy with me, patients move into group therapy at the appropriate time, usually after 6 to 9 months of individual therapy. I have been, and will continue to be, your individual therapist, as well as your group therapist.

Pt. But I'd still see you individually, too, is that right?

Dr. Yes, for a while. The third step might involve working only in the group. So it would really be individual therapy first, then individual with the group, and then the group alone, until the work that brought you to therapy is brought to a reasonable close, satisfactory to you. How does what I am saying sound to you?

Pt. What do you think we can accomplish in group therapy that we're not doing in individual? I have a little bit of apprehension about going into a group.

Dr. Sure. A lot of people do. Actually, some people have comfort in group and apprehension in individual therapy. Different people have varying responses.

Pt. Oh, really?

Dr. Yes. I think there's a universal social anxiety, generally. It doesn't matter who a person is. Just moving into a group creates a kind of anxiety for many people.

Pt. Yeah. I do smaller, I do better in smaller groups, I think, though, so I have some concern. And all these people already know each other, right? I would just be coming in new.

Dr. Yes. The groups that we're talking about are frequently referred to as continuous groups. They are open groups, meaning that from time to time where appropriate, a new member may be added to the group.

About group size: I prefer not to have a group larger than 11, preferably no more than 9. There may be as few as 3 or 4. The exact number is not crucial but is not expected to be larger than 9. The group that we're thinking about your joining is likely to have between 6 and 9 members with a rather stable membership. I don't tend to add more than 1 or 2 members every year or two because we spend a fair amount of time, as you and I have done, getting a sense of how to work together in the kind of individual therapy that we've been doing, and also in the kind of group that you'd be going into. So there aren't usually any big surprises, and there shouldn't be cause for anxiety, other than that which people have when doing something new or meeting new people.

Pt. Won't they resent having a new person come into their group?

Dr. Perhaps, sometimes some unconscious, or even conscious, resentment may be experienced. It's like a sibling who becomes aware that there's going to be a new baby in the family. The parents pay attention to how to help that child, or, in this case, help the group members feel that the new addition will be an addition that will help them all get nourished better, rather than to feel that there will be less time or some loss for the members.

Pt. Well, what do I have to know about going into the group? It's all such a new experience. I don't really know what I'm supposed to do or how I'm supposed to act.

Dr. Do you mean in addition to the things we've talked about from time to time, such as the contractual kinds of understandings?

Pt. Well, yeah, but maybe we could go over that too, since we're talking about going into a group really soon.

Dr. Yes. I think that's a good idea. You've probably read several of my articles that I passed along to you about contracts and group psychotherapy, and a related one that I wrote about extra-group fraternizing and group psychotherapy. But I think we should take some time to review what we've talked about in recent weeks or months about the elements of the contract, by which I mean the agreement. This agreement is not necessarily a written one, but a verbal one between you and me, having to do with the group that we have been talking about your joining pretty soon, possibly in the next few weeks. I've already begun to talk more or less definitely with members of one group in particular, although nothing specific has been revealed, except that it looks likely that we will have a new member joining in the next few weeks. Of course, they'll have adequate notice and so will you, so that everyone will feel more comfortable.

Pt. So they won't be completely surprised by my just showing up?

Dr. No, the members of the group will not be taken by surprise. It's my practice to prepare group members because I don't think it's a good idea for people to be surprised about things of such importance.

Pt. I don't want to be a party crasher or something in a group that already exists.

Dr. Yes. I can well understand that you feel you are a "gate crasher" with people who you believe know each other well and might resent you. Sometimes it can feel a little like that. We talked about a few different groups that I run in which you would certainly work well and in which your therapy goals would probably be well met. We're finally settling on this one particular group that I think makes the best sense based upon age, background, socioeconomics, and the kind of language that's spoken. I think that you will probably find the best fit and they with you in that particular group.

Pt. Okay.

Dr. Of course, any decision we make about joining a group isn't set in stone. We will be flexible. I listen carefully to what I hear from you, and I want to be sure things sound clear from me to you as well. I've found that some people say that having been in an effective psychotherapy group is the best experience they've ever had in their life. I would expect it to be an outstanding experience for everybody. I certainly wish that for you. I think the group experience will permit you to continue to pursue the goals that we've begun to work on that you originally brought into therapy. Those goals generally have to do with basic self-esteem and relationship issues that you experience in your work and personal life, things which are sometimes associated with mild depression, even some heightened anxiety, lowered self-assurance and self-confidence. You doubt yourself even when you know you have high skills and don't think you are actualizing them. Does that seem to fit pretty closely with your understanding?

Pt. Yeah, that's the kind of thing we've been talking about.

Dr. Yes. So you are in agreement with what I am proposing for your joining the group?

Pt. But I'm not really clear about how going into a group will help that sort of thing. I feel like my self-esteem is sort of really on the line in a situation like that. You know, I feel very vulnerable and the idea of a group situation where I don't really know the people ... Do you know what I'm saying? Like with you, we've established kind of a relationship, and I feel like we talk about a lot of things, and you wouldn't do anything to hurt me or be destructive. But these are people I don't know, and I feel like it's hard to trust what might happen there.

Dr. That alliance that you describe between you and me, which is called the therapeutic alliance, is, of course, important. I should point out that not all therapists think one has to have a therapeutic alliance. I think such an alliance essentially means that we speak the same language. I took the model that we're talking about here from an Eastern psychotherapy organization, the Postgraduate Center in New York, that does a lot of group therapy practice and training. This three-step model initially resembles the developing mother/child relationship. After the connection with the mother is established, and a good alliance exists, the child moves on into preschool or kindergarten. The mother is still there at that point. There's not just the child with the mother, but the child in the social situation as well. Eventually, the child lives, as most of us do, largely in the social world thereafter. That's pretty much the model that I use here in combined therapy: individual, individual and group, and then group. Of course, there is some anxiety in all transitions. I think that is what you and I are dealing with now. It's important that you talk about these feelings that you have. I would like you to feel as comfortable as possible, knowing that all will be all right. The group will be safe, a good holding place, a kind of a sanctuary. Gradually you will develop a sense of increasing comfort, trust, and safety within it. It will be a good place for you to continue your therapeutic work. You may have discovered that, at times, I function as a mirror for you; the group functions like a tailor's mirror, a three-way mirror, where you can see yourself from multiple perspectives.

Pt. Oh, yeah. I see what you're saying.

Dr. Yes. You can get a look at yourself from a lot of different angles. The poet Robert Burns said what amounts to, "I wish that I had the gift to see myself as others do." That's probably the most cited group therapy quote. Many people don't have a sense of themselves as experienced by others. That's what a meaningful group therapy experience provides.

Pt. That's really the hardest thing to get, isn't it, to see yourself as other people see you?

Dr. It can be difficult because people often don't want to hurt others' feelings, or they may dissemble, or hold things in, not telling people quite how they feel. But in a therapy group, where people are encouraged to express their sincere feelings, the members can be the beneficiaries of accurate, valuable insights and feedback from the other members.

Pt. So what if I go into this group and nobody likes me?

Dr. Well, it's not likely that'll happen, because you're 47 years old and you've had a couple of marriages, that were satisfying in different ways each for a period of time. You've now been single for over a decade. You live very well in the world of others in many, many ways. You're always in groups, if you stop to think about it. Since you were little, you were in some form of group. Some people just don't think of themselves as skilled in groups. But they're in groups, nonetheless. Whether they're sports groups, church groups, athletic groups, people are in all kinds of groups.

Pt. Well, I guess all through school and so forth, you're in groups of different types. Or your work colleagues and so on. I do have to confess to feelings of anxiety about being in group. I feel that it puts me in a very vulnerable situation. I can't really describe why that is, but it does seem as if you can't go into your, go into the group in the same way as your group of colleagues at work, and so forth.

Dr. Of course, your awareness of those anxieties is an important recognition.

Pt. And you sort of have an obligation to be more open and yet I'm not sure I'm always convinced that's the best way to behave with people.

Dr. Yes. And it's important to remember that there's no urgency. And should you feel unduly uncomfortable, we certainly can wait. There's no requirement to join the group this week or the next or ever at all, actually. This is an important decision, and the way we proceed must make sense to you.

Pt. But I suppose it never will feel comfortable till I go ahead and start doing it. I mean, is that true?

Dr. I think that there'll be a readiness that you'll experience and that you'll feel it's a good time to begin. I think that's what you've been saying recently, which is why we are reviewing this now. The courage and fortitude you are alluding to is an important recognition. Your awareness of this need is a positive sign. It is one of the indications that to me suggests you are ready to enter a group.

Pt. So why do you think I might be ready now?

Dr. I think it's a natural progression from what you've been dealing with in therapy with me individually, with matters pertaining to how you see and experience yourself. And it seems to me that a group of dispassionate others will add a lot. People who are compatriots, fellow colleagues, people who are in similar situations, can broaden and deepen the experiences you already have gained with me.

Pt. Well, I suppose, too, I mean, I have the thought that being in a group, the other people in the group, I suppose, don't feel any particular obligation to me, so, I mean I guess I would say whatever their responses to me are, they should be straightforward and valid, right? Because they don't have any reason not to be.

Dr. In theory, that sounds good. We can never be sure of the motives and aspirations of any other person, but part of what happens in a group is that, after a period of time, we get to see the patterns, not only yours but those of others too. That's one of the reasons why regularity and continuity is so important. We get a sense of whether what they're saying sounds like it fits and is true. So over a period of time it would be difficult for anybody to fake responses or to hold back significantly.

Pt. Certainly not the whole group anyway, right?

Dr. Of course. That's the value of having a number of people, because of the diverse responses. There's a kind of distilling experience which occurs.

Pt. Well, how long, typically, does a person stay in a group?

Dr. That can vary. In psychodynamic groups such as we're talking about here, where we use words to describe what's going on in our lives, many people think, and I agree, that it may take as long as 6 months to feel like you speak the language of the group. These are verbal groups with pretty high–functioning adults.

Pt. So that makes sense.

Dr. I don't think it makes a lot of sense to think that anything less than a year represents a significant amount of group psychotherapy in such a group. That's not always the case, but something like that. Sometimes group therapy may extend for many years as some people discover things as they move along that they need to or wish to work on. Some people don't get all their psychotherapy needs met at once either; sometimes they will participate in a group psychotherapy group and complete much of their work, and, for one reason or another, may bring that work to a close and then continue at another time, for other reasons or to deepen their experiences. In other words, the psychotherapy group is not just a support group; it's not just to make you feel good but to help you. The kind of group we've been talking about is exploratory, insight-oriented, and one that asks you to be self-reflective and curious about yourself.

Pt. I suppose it's like our therapy, doesn't necessarily make you feel good after every session.

Dr. Yes, of course. In fact, it's been said, and I think it's true, that if you always feel good in your psychotherapy group, you're probably in a support group. It's typical of support groups to get people to feel good most of the time. That is their intended purpose. Such groups tend to be shorter-termed, for example, post-train wreck, post-divorce, etc. They make use of the concept of bridging where people in the group help each other recognize that they share a number of matters in common, they feel good about that, and they look forward to it. However, in the psychodynamic group such as the one we're talking about, while it's not our intention to cause pain any more than it's a dentist's intention to make your tooth hurt when he probes a nerve, the experience of exploration may sometimes cause you to feel uncomfortable. But it's unlikely for you to feel any real loss or casualty or anything of the sort. Such losses occurred to you many, many years ago. But you might experience, or I might say reexperience, some familiar pains. Sometimes, feedback evokes feelings which may cause you to feel discomfort and even pain. This should not be equated with injury, harm, or casualty.

Pt. I think I understand. What else do I need to know about going into the group?

Dr. Of course, there are thoughts that will occur to you as you approach your first group session. But it makes sense to review the contract. The contract is important because it gives people something to draw upon when things are unclear. And there's only one reason one ever needs a contract, Mary, and that's to interpret deviations from it. That can be true for a marital contract or for any contract for that matter. One cannot unilaterally change elements of a contract. Penalties are always imposed when one unilaterally decides to change what has been agreed upon, whether a MasterCard arrangement, a car payment, a mortgage payment, or an agreement with friends.

Pt. Sure. Just like in the legal profession.

Dr. Yes. And you, as an expert attorney, would certainly know what that's like. Although I have no expertise as a lawyer, my understanding is that it's very similar. In the contract that makes sense for you and me, let's review the elements we need to be clear about. These are really not rules. In fact, there's only one rule I insist upon in this or any group I am associated with: at no time is any person permitted to hurt himself or herself, physically or emotionally. That's the only rule. The other things we'll talk about are elements of the contract (nowadays also known as agreement), rather than rules. Make sense so far?

Pt. Okay. Sure.

Dr. I think you will bring much that will be of value to the group—as—a—whole, although your goal isn't to be helpful to the group. Your goal is to get your treatment needs met. We do that using the group process. But we're not treating the group, we're treating you.

Pt. Yes. But I like to think I could offer something.

Dr. Yes. I know that you do. This is an important consideration I make for bringing anyone new into a group. As the people in the group get to know you, they will recognize this too. I'm quite certain it won't take long. It's important to know that the group we're talking about meets Wednesday nights, from 5:00 to 7:00 in the evening. This happens to be a 2-hour group, although some of the groups that I lead are $1^{1}/_{2}$ hours. The group meets in this room. Members in the group understand that they're expected to be on time for all sessions and to stay throughout the group for each session. On those occasions when I take vacations, I try to let the group know as much in advance as possible, to minimize any disruption. In this particular group, a process known as the alternate group, meaning the group meeting without the leader, frequently occurs. So, even if I'm out of town, the group sometimes meets. Lest that be of any concern to you, please understand that if it looks like the people in it are not comfortable, or that it doesn't seem well advised, there's no reason that we *have* to do that. But the group typically has met and functions quite smoothly and comfortably.

Pt. Okay.

Dr. Every Wednesday. Does that sound okay?

Pt. Yeah. That's fine. Well, if you're not going to be here, you know ahead of time.

Dr. I want to be sure you are clear about the time structure and can agree with it.

Pt. Yes. Sure, that time's okay for me.

Dr. Okay. Great. Another element of the group that we need to discuss is that this is a therapeutic group, not a social group. In other words, people are here for psychotherapeutic reasons and not to develop friends. It *does* happen that strong feelings occur while you're in the group, and you might feel very friendly, or sometimes maybe the opposite. Sometimes you might want to extend your contacts beyond the group session.

Pt. Uh-huh.

Dr. I am referring to opportunities to meet for coffee or drinks, to fix houses, to go to weddings, bar mitzvahs, and that sort of thing. It's important to pay careful attention to boundaries. We've frequently discussed in individual therapy the crucial need for meticulous scrutiny of boundaries.

Pt. Right.

Dr. And while it's certainly understandable that people want to take material out of the group, it makes sense that all work be done wherever possible within this room, in the consultation room, which is where I consider that group psychotherapy takes place. Many important contacts may occur in the waiting room or in the hallway, and so forth, but those don't constitute group psychotherapy. Those are not activities I observe. You are paying me to be an expert observer about events that we together can see. In group therapy, that's referred to as equal access, where all of us equally have an opportunity to observe behavior that's occurring among us. But if members take behavior outside the group, then we're sort of relegated to hearing third-hand stories, frequently distorted, about what occurred. And I don't think you need to pay me to listen to somebody's accounting of what occurred.

Pt. So you mean whatever interactions we have, they should really occur here, and not someplace else, is that what you are saying?

Dr. Well, it's not a rule and it's not really a "should," but it's an element of the contract. My clinical experience and extensive research in group psychotherapy show that, at least in this kind of work, it's best when all members in the group can observe what's going on right in front of us in the treatment room. Other experienced group therapists agree with this understanding. If I had my wish, I would prefer that somehow, in a magical way, at the beginning of the group, a helicopter would drop everybody into the room comfortably and at the end of it would remove everybody. People would then use the experiences they discovered during the group and extrapolate those learnings to people not in the group. Group members agree to keep the group sacrosanct, a special trusted place that they don't violate, so that they can develop the level of intimacy crucial to do the work needed.

Pt. Uh-huh. I understand.

Dr. Now, Mary, closely related to the element of the contract that the group is a therapeutic group, not a social group, is the issue of confidentiality. Members in the group understand that at no time do members talk about issues outside of the group with people not in the group or about anything that in any way identifies a group member. That's crucial for patients to develop a sense of safety, like peeling off layers of an onion, to get to deeper, more important, delicate and vulnerable feelings that people are sometimes hesitant or resistant to explore.

Pt. So, the kinds of things I would say in the group, other people won't talk about to other people?

Dr. Well, I can't say that they won't, but they agree not to do so. You can only go so far in this world to tell people the things that are expected and to create agreements and contracts. It should be obvious to you, as a lawyer, that I don't have any way of controlling somebody when they're not in this room.

Pt. No, of course.

Dr. Initially, we must take people at their stated word. That's why, I think, developing a sense of deepening intimacy takes a little bit of time. Don't feel hurried to do anything before you want to. And when the time feels right to you, you'll say the things that are important. That's why some therapists say that in group psychotherapy, work doesn't actually get done until patients begin telling their secrets. But I consider each person in a group to be his or her own chairperson, and so please say whatever it is you wish whenever you want, as soon as you want. I'm not likely to ask you to say something that you haven't said or don't want to say. I expect that when you're ready or want us to know, you'll say your thing. And the group is also a place where you can't be forced to say what you don't want to say. That's another reason I'm there, to make sure it's fair and safe. I won't let anybody be abusive or punishing to you or demand that you say something when you say you don't want to.

Pt. See, because I feel you and I have a relationship and I could say anything to you. You wouldn't go out and repeat it to other people, but I don't know who these people are, and I suppose they don't have that kind of professional obligation. But I suppose when I get to know them, maybe I would feel differently.

Dr. I would hope for that, and I would expect that. My experience typically bears that out. It is true that they don't have the professional obligation that I do, but they sort of share the same ethos that I espouse. They've all had the same discussion with me that you and I are now having, and they understand and have agreed to it. Now we've talked about confidentiality and its significance. Closely related is the concept of extra-group fraternizing, that is, social contacts outside of the group with group members or the therapist. And now, Mary, let's discuss this issue a bit more fully. I apologize if this seems so wordy, even a bit of a lecture, rather than a discussion, at the moment. But it's so important to be clear about this phenomenon.

Pt. Right. And I really want to know what it's all about, and what I'm getting into.

Dr. Of course. The extra-group fraternizing element suggests, and again it's not a rule, but an *understanding* that group work is best done in our consultation room. And when people do, either wittingly or unwittingly, have outside-the-group contact, it becomes the mandate of each member to report back as soon as possible to the group the nature of the contact. In that way, we can observe together what exactly went on, ensuring equal access. So, this helps us understand any changes in the interpersonal relationships between those involved. Is this clear to you?

Pt. Yeah, I think so.

Dr. All right. So we understand that we do our work in the group room, and as we have previously discussed, we understand that such behavior may involve acting out, when members take something out of the group without the other group members knowing about it. That goes along with the other elements we talked about: therapeutic group, not social group; and confidentiality. It becomes clear, then, that extra-group fraternizing represents a matter of considerable importance. Now, I do have some esteemed colleagues whom I respect highly and who operate differently. They often encourage contact with their patients according to a different rationale. This isn't a comment for or against them. Sometimes in different settings, such as inpatient group psychotherapy, extra-group frater-

nizing is not only unavoidable but often therapeutic. But most psychodynamic group psychotherapists that I know dealing with outpatient
groups, such as what we're doing here, operate according to the framework I'm describing. So, we've discussed the following elements of the
contract: meeting here Wednesday 5:00 to 7:00; the group as a therapeutic group, not a social group; confidentiality; and extra-group fraternizing. Do you have any questions about these?

Pt. No, that sounds fine. That sounds fine. I'm a little apprehensive, but I'm
up for it.

Dr. Do these things make sense to you, and do you feel comfortable agreeing to them?

Pt. Yes. Yes. All of that makes sense to me.

Dr. All right. Then let's discuss another element. This is a verbal group, not
an action group. So, in this particular group, patients are asked to put
their feelings into words, not into action.

Pt. So you mean we won't hit each other, right?

Dr. Oh, for sure, we wouldn't expect any of that. But there are groups that
are action groups, in which members are asked to put their experiences
into action and not into words. We happen to use a different approach,
again not better or worse, but this is the way that we function: it's a verbal, not an action group. Any tendency to action, or possibly even acting out, would be important to put into words.

Pt. Okay. Well, being a small person, I'm more comfortable with words than
action anyway. (Laughs.)

Dr. Yes. Well, you may discover yourself to be bigger than you think. (Patient
laughs.) I think another element that's sometimes hard to grasp at first is
that members are encouraged to interrupt whenever they want. The word
"interrupt" may be an unfortunate one in our language. Here, members
understand and agree to say whatever they want, whenever they want, at
any time, not cleansing or editing, and trusting to the group process to
make sense of things as they come out. In our group's context, it is better to interrupt, even though it may sometimes feel socially awkward to
do so, than to keep things in too long, waiting for a proper time to say
things, doing all the work internally. There will probably be some tendency to do that anyway because you're human. But if you could just
blurt stuff out spontaneously, gradually trusting to the group process,
you'll see what sense can be derived from our free associations.

Pt. But how can you have a discussion if people are interrupting each other?

Dr. Well, we're not really just having a discussion. You need to recognize
that we are not talking about everyday conversations, for example, in
your law office or in a public forum. We're trying to make sense of the
ways in which we relate and so it isn't a discussion group but a group

of people with bubbling-over experiences. Freud said that the unconscious is a seething cauldron that never sleeps. It just bubbles over. I think we shouldn't try to put partitions on soup; rather, just keep stirring it, sample it, and dip the spoon in wherever we wish.

Pt. Okay, I'll try to remember that.

Dr. Does it make sense? Is that okay and something you can agree to?

Pt. Yes, I can agree to it.

Dr. All right. Now another important element which is difficult to nail down specifically is that patients coming into this group agree to stay in the group until the reasons bringing them into the group are done with. Basically, this rationale says that you have your issues to work on and that you agree to stay with them until things are pretty well eased and clarified.

Pt. I guess so. I guess I'm not exactly sure what that means in this case.

Dr. Of course, we're never really sure ahead of time what it means. It may help you to understand that if somebody comes in to group and thinks that a week or two later all's well, that's probably not the case. So the members agree to stay with the group even if they feel a little frustrated or troubled; they agree not to just change course on themselves and the group precipitously.

Pt. Well, we'd talk about it anyway, right, if there were some problems?

Dr. Of course. This element suggests that we'd not only talk about it, but that you would see it through and stay with it, in addition to talking about it. Stay with it until your treatment issues are completed.

Pt. Okay, I guess I understand now.

Dr. Does this sound acceptable?

Pt. I guess so.

Dr. What I have been telling you is not meant to be coercive.

Pt. No, well, I'm sure I'll understand that better when I get involved in the group.

Dr. It's important that you understand it clearly now. Or before you get in the group. Of course, by "now," I don't mean today.

Pt. What if I get into the group and I find that it's a really, really uncomfortable situation?

Dr. You may find it uncomfortable at times.

Pt. What if it makes me feel miserable?

Dr. You may at times feel bothered.

Pt. Well, I guess I'm not saying now and then. Would we be able to discuss that?

Dr. Yes, and that's why we will continue to meet individually and, if need be, even extra, if we need to, but I don't anticipate that. You'll do just fine. Everything's quite on course.

Pt. I guess based on what you know, you're not expecting that would be a situation in which I'm miserable or really very overly uncomfortable, right?

Dr. I can see your being uncomfortable, but I think that's grist for the mill and that's group material and perfectly workable within the group.

Pt. I see. I mean, you've chosen this particular group based on our relationship and what we've already discussed, is that right?

Dr. Well, yes, I think it's the best fit.

Pt. Okay.

Dr. Yes, and not just a good fit, but the best one for you. I'm very hopeful and encouraged about the possibilities for the work that you'll continue doing in that group.

Pt. Okay, well, I think you have better judgment in that area than I.

Dr. Well, what we want to be sure about now is not just my judgment but whether the things that I'm saying to you in terms of the elements of the contract are clear and whether you agree to them.

Pt. I just don't know in terms of agreeing in the future. I guess it's hard to agree when you don't understand what the future's supposed to be, how you can agree to something, not knowing what it is.

Dr. I understand your concern.

Pt. But I do understand that you don't believe there's any reason to have anxiety about that, I mean, and I accept that and I respect your judgment about that so I guess, in theory, I can agree.

Dr. Well, it's important to agree in more than theory, in practice, because you're going to be entering a group that has people in it who are expecting that members will be there, stay there, and will work things through, and who won't in any way surprise them with sudden exits based upon an interpretation or a feeling of the moment.

Pt. Oh, of the moment? Well, if that's what you're asking, I think I can agree to that. I'm certainly willing to give everything due consideration, I think, and not respond to some particular specific event. So, if that's what we're talking about—

Dr. Yes. What we're talking about is that you agree to stay in the group until the reasons that brought you into therapy and into the therapy group are actually dealt with. Not just to give consideration to it, that's certainly assumed, but to stay in the group until you're done with your work. I know that this may seem vague. I don't know how to make it more specific. I'll have a sense about how things are going for you. And so will you.

Pt. Well, if it's an issue of a mutual decision, I think I can agree to that.

Dr. But if you're not certain, that's not actually an agreement.

Pt. You know, as a lawyer, it's hard for me to agree to something in the future that's not something specified.

Dr. That is one of the reasons you came to me for therapy in the first place, wasn't it? To experience parts of yourself that you are not certain about, the nonprofessional parts of yourself, the emotional parts, for example. I know that in your work as a lawyer you find it hard to work with others generally and to permit them to structure a situation.

Pt. Well, I have to, I have to consider the various contingencies that could arise.

Dr. But I am not treating a lawyer. I am treating somebody that has described lower self-esteem and poor relationships in many parts of her life, long before she was ever a lawyer.

Pt. Well, that's true. That's certainly true. What else do we need to talk about?

Dr. Well, I don't know that we've agreed to anything with respect to this element yet.

Pt. But let's look at the other issues and we can come back to that.

Dr. I think it's important to stay with this for the moment. The other elements are not directly related to this one. But this element can sometimes seem puzzling. People coming into the group agree to stay with the group until the reasons that brought them there are dealt with.

Pt. Okay, so you're saying, in other words, to agree to stay in the group until we've, until we've addressed those issues, is that right?

Dr. Yes. Well, not just addressed them, we'll be addressing them all along, but until they're treated. Until you're making better sense of them in your life.

Pt. Okay.

Dr. Is that okay with you?

Pt. Yeah.

Dr. We've talked about where the group meets, Mary, and that it's a therapeutic and not a social group. We've talked about confidentiality and extra-group fraternizing. We've talked about this being a verbal group, not an action group. We've talked about interrupting and putting feelings into the moment. We've talked about staying with your issues until they're brought to completion or closure.

Pt. Right.

Dr. We should also pay attention to fee responsibility and who would be paying for the therapy. As we discussed, the fee for this group is $X per month.

Pt. Right.

Dr. This fee is paid monthly, and patients pay a month in advance besides that when they begin. It's like paying a security deposit, although it's not exactly that. So, as you begin group, let us say next month, at the beginning of the month, you would pay the monthly fee, and you would pay for one month extra at that point. Then at the end of the next month, you would pay for one month, which would be for the next following month. This arrangement may help buy time for the patient and/or the group in the unlikely event of a sudden, premature termination from the group. If we can, in this way, encourage the patient to remain for the four or five weeks (or eight to ten treatment hours) of that month, it is often possible to work through whatever impulsive or acting-out aspects may be involved. There are, of course, no guarantees, but I've discovered that such an arrangement serves to protect the patient and the group.

Pt. Okay. I understand.

Dr. Does that make sense to you?

Pt. Sure. Right.

Dr. And you would be paying me directly? There are no relatives or third parties in this case?

Pt. Oh, yes. It's my own funds.

Dr. All right. Should there be any reason for anybody else to be involved, then you and I would talk about what issues might arise with respect to disclosing information pertaining to your treatment.

Pt. Okay.

Dr. Basically, I think that would be pretty much it. That's essentially the whole contract that I find helps us in the group. I haven't got much more to add at the moment, or to delete. I think this will help to keep things clear for you. The elements of the contract are intended to provide a clear structure to facilitate your therapeutic work in the group. I am confident that this discussion will help to smooth your entry into the group.

Pt. Okay. Great. So then I'll start the first Wednesday of next month, right?

Dr. Do these things sound clear? Do you agree to them?

Pt. Yes. Yes.

Dr. I think the Wednesday night group makes sense. Why don't we start on the first Wednesday of next month?

Pt. Okay.

Dr. Fine. And I would like to add a recommendation.

Pt. What's that?

Dr. This is sometimes hard to remember, but it's worthwhile. When you come into the group, it's such a special moment. Imagine yourself being a little fly on your shoulder, watching yourself as you're in the group. You know, we've talked about the observing ego, watching ourselves as we function, keeping an eye on ourselves. Developing an observing ego is an important function of maturity. And entering a new group, particularly such a special one as this, is so rare in life, you can't ever get it again. You can only have one first moment entering a new group. Even though you may have anxieties and concerns, try to use a little energy to pay attention to what it's like for you, perhaps just before you come in, or during that day, or in the waiting room, or as soon as you enter the group room, and then what it's like for you during that session. If you can be that little fly on your shoulder, pay special attention not to lose that very special, virgin moment, that can never be had again. There's only one first first.

Pt. Okay, I'll try to remember —

Dr. Yes. I know I've been saying a lot. It may be difficult to remember all of this. But I can assure you that it will make more sense as soon as you're there. You will see people that are within 10 or 15 years of your age, men and women, married, single, most all of them with college-plus education, and coming from various socioeconomic backgrounds. But they all talk the same language and have pretty much the same interests. It's a rare occasion in life to be in a place where you can assume that the people in that room, unlike most places in our world, are willing to listen to just about anything you have to say, for two hours, every week. No matter what.

Pt. It sounds exciting.

Dr. Yes. Very exciting.

Pt. Thank you.

Dr. I'm delighted. I'm looking forward to it. I think you'll be an asset to the group. Are there things you want to ask? That's probably an inhibiting question in itself. Anything you want to ask that I didn't touch on? I've been exhaustive, actually exhausting, probably.

Pt. Well, I don't have any questions right now, but I guess if I think of anything in the meantime, we can always talk about it next week, right?

Dr. Of course. We have several weeks left. All sounds fine, and I think we're all set. I'm looking forward to your joining the group and, with your permission, I will begin to be a little more specific with them next week. I will let them know that we'll have a new person. No details, of course, will be disclosed, although they may ask questions. This group has learned not to even do much of that. They'll likely just say, "We'll wait," and be curious and let the fantasies roam. They've learned to be able to wait and work with their feelings and thoughts. The group will be eager to meet you.

Pt. Okay. Good. I'm looking forward to the opportunity.

Dr. That's great. And we'll see you next week.

Pt. Okay. Bye.

Dr. Goodbye, Mary.

ADDENDUM

The above interview is a simulated, condensed assessment and preparation for group psychotherapy conducted with an actor, Mary, who plays the role of a patient who has been in individual psychotherapy with me once weekly for 10 months for treatment of depression. Our continuing treatment plan, which is on schedule, is to have her join a specific one of my adult, continuous (open) outpatient psychodynamic psychotherapy groups. Primary areas of focus deal with her chronic pervasive sense of low self-esteem and associated mild depression and anxiety, with special attention's being paid to her less-than-fulfilling interpersonal and occupational relationships and fears of intimacy, which are at the core of her resistances.

In the previous months, and particularly in the three-session consultation for psychotherapy which I typically conduct when first meeting a patient, a complete history was taken. The simulated assessment above assumes that historical background and knowledge. Typical information I find helpful includes a complete family and medical history, the latter detailing all significant illnesses, hospitalizations, allergies and surgeries, sleep and eating habits, athletic routines, use of alcohol, caffeine, and all prescription and nonprescription medications. Educational, social, sexual, religious, civic, recreational, vocational, financial, and legal histories are detailed. Tendencies toward impulsivity and acting out are noted, as are the patient's group experiences from early childhood on, both successes and failures. An evaluation of the patient's chief complaints, symptoms, goals, objectives, present and past experiences with the psychotherapies, and fantasies, hopes, and expectations for the anticipated therapy are discussed. Since patients usually are referred to me for psychotherapy generally, it is my practice to inform such prospective patients during those early first sessions that, should we decide to work together, I conduct psychotherapy groups, and it is likely that later in treatment, but probably not before nine months, a psychotherapy group (led by me or someone else) may be indicated. This assessment, then, is the natural evolution of psychotherapy begun almost a year earlier, and it is assumed for assessment purposes here that I have considered issues of selection and group composition for balance and to create the most nourishing environment for the patient.

CHAPTER 7

Record Keeping

JOHN R. PRICE AND A. RAE PRICE

Joe had said he'd "try" group. In response to clients who enter on this basis, I ask them to commit to a minimum of four months before they leave group. Joe, a former business owner, was managerial in group even to the point of challenging the therapist with such statements as "I wouldn't do it that way."

After seven weeks in group, he said group wasn't doing anything for him (not that he wasn't working the group) and he had decided to quit. In response to my reminding him of his four-month contract, he said that he had never agreed to such a thing. Moral: therapists have a less than 100% success rate in predicting successful group members.

TRACKING THE STAGES OF REFERRALS

Since you may be at various stages of referring your clients in individual therapy to group therapy, it can be helpful to maintain a flow chart. This chart is in addition to whatever entries you make in the client's individual folder. A chart can be as simple as columns on $1/4''$ graph paper or you can create a layout with your computer (see Table II). In any event, these six column headings seem to work: "Client's Name," "Mentioned," "Discussed," "Yes," "Group," and "Will Start." Following is a suggested approach to accomplish this often complex system of referrals:

Table II   Keeping Track of Referrals

Name	Mentioned	Discussed	Yes	Group	Will Start
Anthony, Susan B.	1/25/98	1/31/98	1/31/98	Tu 5:30	2/07/98
Washington, Martha (with George)	2/07/98				
Madison, James (with Dolly)	2/24/98	3/07/98	5/04/98	Th Noon	6/01/98
Freud, Sigmund	2/28/98	3/21/98	4/24/98	Th 3:30	6/01/98
Roosevelt, Eleanor	3/03/98	4/13/98	5/02/98	We 5:30	5/10/98
Einstein, Albert S.	3/24/98	4/07/98	4/07/98	Th 3:30	5/11/98
Addams, Jane	4/06/98	4/13/98	4/20/98	Th 3:30	5/11/98
Tudor, Elizabeth	4/12/98	4/19/98	4/26/98	Th 3:30	5/11/98
Tubman, Harriet	5/02/98	5/18/98	5/30/98	Tu 5:30	6/06/98
Antoinette, Marie		5/02/98	5/02/98	Th 3:30	5/18/98
Keller, Helen		1/23/98	5/05/98	Th 3:30	5/11/98
Lincoln, Abraham (with Mary)	5/09/98	5/23/98		Th Noon	
Mead, Margaret	5/11/98	5/19/98	5/19/98	Mo 3:30	5/29/98
Curie, Marie (with Pierre)	5/12/98	5/23/98	5/25/98	Th 3:30	6/01/98
Dickinson, Emily		5/12/98		Mo 5:30	
Washington, Booker T.	5/12/98				
Tudor, Henry (with Anne)		5/12/98	5/23/98	Tu 5:30	5/30/98
Van Gogh, Vincent		5/19/98	5/19/98	Th 3:30	5/25/98
Stowe, Harriet B.	5/30/98			Th Noon	

Thus, if you have, say, five clients in various stages of the referral process, using the flow chart, you can keep track of where you are with each client. You only need enter the date when you "mentioned" group therapy, the date when you "discussed," and so forth. You will probably find this much easier than relying on either your memory or notations in the client's folder. This charting also keeps you focused on getting your individual clients into group.

The process of recording *all* of the dates at which various steps in the referral are taking place makes for maximum efficiency in tracking the referral process—for *all* potential participants.

KEEPING TRACK OF TREATMENT

In addition to any entries you may wish to make in a client's folder, it is helpful to maintain a folder for each therapy group. You might dictate or write notes following each therapy session on the various clients who "worked" in that session. Particularly if you have several groups, this form of notetaking serves to remind you, in advance of a session, who worked on what during the previous session. You may well want to make more extensive notes in the client's individual folder.

Both for tracking client attendance in group and for billing purposes, another flow chart can be created for each of the your groups. Following is an easy—and obvious—layout for keeping track of attendance.

Table III   Keeping Track of Attendance

NAME	Feb 6	Feb 13	Feb 20	Feb 29	Mar 6	Mar 13	Mar 20	Mar 29	Apr 3	Apr 10	Apr 17	Apr 24	May 1	May 8	May 15	May 22	May 29	Jun 5	Jun 12	Jun 19	Jun 26
Charles Dickens	✓		X	✓	✓	✓	✓	✓	✓	X	✓		✓	✓	✓	✓		✓		X	X
Robert Lee	✓		X		✓	✓	X	X	G												
Eli Whitney	X			✓	✓	✓		✓	X	✓	X	X			✓	✓			✓	✓	✓
Edith Wharton	X		X	X	✓	✓	✓	✓	✓		✓	X	✓	✓	X	X					X
Mary Shelley	✓		✓	✓	✓	✓	✓	✓	✓	✓	✓	✓	✓	✓	✓	✓		✓	✓	✓	✓
Clara Barton	✓		X	✓	✓	X	✓	✓	✓	X	✓	✓	✓	✓	✓	✓		✓	✓	✓	X
Richard Strauss	✓		✓	✓		X			X	✓	✓	✓	X	✓		✓		✓	✓	✓	X
Claude Monet	✓		✓	✓	✓	✓	✓	✓	✓	✓	------NC------			✓	✓			✓	X	X	✓
Aaron Burr																		1st	✓	✓	✓

Note: AGPA: Group didn't meet (February); MEMORIAL DAY (May).

Down the left-hand side of either a sheet of graph paper or a computer lay-out, list the clients' names; across the top, enter the dates of the group sessions and the month for, say, a six- to eight-month period. In the column for any given therapy date, a check mark indicating the client's attendance tells the secretary to put the charge on the client's insurance form. An "X" indicating a cancellation or a blank indicating a no-show tells the secretary to bill the client separately for the absence. A "G" indicates graduation from group.

You gave clients a copy of your ground rules when you discussed the pos-sibility of going into group therapy. Therein, you told them that charges are on a monthly basis. You also told them that in those months that have five ther-apy sessions, they will not be billed for the fifth session.

You also told them that missed sessions cannot be billed to the insurance company. As each client is paying for a reserved slot in a group, each is expected to pay for missed sessions. This distinction is important not only for the client but also for the secretary or billing service.

In the orientation, in addition to telling the client that charges are on a monthly basis, you gave the client a handout, "An Introduction to Group Psy-chotherapy" (see Appendix B). At the outset, arrange with the client how to handle payment or copayment.

You may wish to offer the client the possibility of charging his copay or out-of-pocket expense on a credit card. Some therapists request payment for the month in advance, thereby simplifying the whole billing procedure. As a new group therapist, how do you set fees for group? Here are two possibilities. One, if you know of group therapists in your general area, you may wish to phone their offices to ask what they charge. Also, you can call the American Group Psychotherapy Association for information about the nearest affiliate society in your area. (See "Helpful Names and Addresses" in Appendix A.)

CHAPTER 8

The Group or Client's First Session

JOHN R. PRICE AND DAVID R. HESCHELES

I was an early trainee and had eight patients in one group. One time, I appeared for group and no one showed up. I was alone in the room and decided I would just wait. Five minutes before the end, one patient walked in.

When the word got around, and it did, that I had waited, the others came back, little by little. And I had a group.

Techniques for beginning the first psychotherapy group session depend on your theoretical orientation and your purposes as a group leader. Also, techniques for introducing a new group member into an established group will vary. In groups such as time-limited Cognitive/Behavioral Focal groups, the client commits for the entire length of the group sessions, and thus introduction of new members into the group is not an issue.

In Psychodynamic groups, preparing the group for a new member is generally more extensive than it is for Eclectic groups. The extent of preparation generally depends, however, on the predilection of the therapist.

COGNITIVE BEHAVIORAL FOCAL GROUPS

Homogeneously focus-oriented groups usually become cohesive more quickly, have fewer conflicts among members, and offer more immediate support that do other kinds of groups. Focal groups are highly structured and strongly goal-oriented. They use homework and structured exercises to promote change. And they have a high educational function.

Before the focal groups begin, you, as the therapist, should have specific, written protocols which detail the objectives, goals, and structured exercises for each session. You should define each concept to the group and to the client and then define the skill each must develop. Thus, members have the opportunity to understand the concept and to practice that skill; they can then practice in the outside world through homework assignments.

1. Before the first session: in the Cognitive Behavioral Focal group, you will want to secure, in a pregroup screening, a sound foundation; you should emphasize to the clients that:

   a. consistent attendance is important
   b. any absences must be discussed beforehand, if at all possible
   c. active work, through structured exercises and homework assignments, is essential to overcome difficulties
   d. clients need to agree to the goals, expectations, and cost of the entire group. Generally, clients pay in advance for the entire number of sessions to ensure attendance and commitment.

The therapist should also determine the client's motivation to work actively on difficulties. If the client, according to the therapist's assessment, is not so motivated at the present time, the therapist may decide to continue seeing the client in individual sessions rather than put the client in a group

2. In the first session, you not only introduce yourself but also have the group members introduce themselves to each other, either through a structured dyadic exercise or through a whole-group exercise.

In a structured dyadic exercise, you ask the group to break into pairs, or dyads; partners in the dyad will share the reasons each decided to join this group and what each expects to change as a result of this group experience. After 10 minutes, each member of the dyad will report to the large group what his partner said.

In the structured whole group exercise, you state, "We are going to have a go-around and each group member will introduce him- or herself by first name, telling one thing about which she or he is most proud and two things she or he will change in this group experience."

3. During the first session, clarify the time and duration of the group session. Also, define the structure of the group, telling the group members that this experience works best as a closed group and that attendance is necessary at all sessions.

Also describe the format of each session: perhaps first some educational talk about a concept, then structured exercises to practice and develop the skills, followed by homework assignments. Finally, establish the goal of this particular therapy group and reiterate the ground rules:

    a. that everything in the psychotherapy group is confidential

    b. that homework assignments must be completed

    c. that there will be no physical contact: hitting inside the group or dating outside the group. Focal group members should know exactly what to expect after the first session. It is up to you, in week-to-week sessions, to provide the structure through the established written protocols.

PSYCHODYNAMIC GROUPS

Before the first session, you need to pay attention to client selection. group composition, and contracting. In client selection, you will want to try for an optimal therapeutic fit. (Refer to "Some Special Considerations for Psychodynamic Groups," Chapter IV.) You will need to determine the motivation and expectancies the client has about the psychotherapy group. You will set specific goals in order to improve the client's ability to express feelings and develop a therapeutic alliance. You will look at fulfilling the social roles which are necessary for a successful group composition.

Group composition is less of an issue in Focal groups and in Eclectic groups than it is in Psychodynamic groups. As they are more homogeneous, Focus groups usually become cohesive more quickly and offer more immediate support.

In Psychodynamic groups, which are more heterogeneous, stages of development are more easily defined, and, therefore, composition plays a greater role. In a homogeneous group, for example, shyness might be the criterion for the group's composition. In heterogeneous groups, the intrapersonal and interpersonal issues of each member take on great importance.

Contracting, or pregroup training, consists of helping to alleviate client's fears, such as fears of being attacked, being embarrassed, or picking up other client's symptoms. Contracting will also help the client understand the interpersonal nature of psychotherapy groups, in such areas as interacting with others, sharing feelings, or expecting positive and supportive feedback about oneself. As the leader, you will also define the rules around confidentiality, extragroup interaction, and boundary issues. "Boundary issues" include having no physical contact, no smoking and eating during sessions, attending regularly, and arriving on time. You, the leader, are generally more active during the first few sessions. Point out similarities between members to promote cohesiveness and trust. In general, you will usually want to interfere with very intimate disclosures by asking the client to save this important revelation until more trust is established in the group. You will also encourage positive feedback during the first few sessions to encourage trust and closeness. More confrontative feedback needs to be saved for later.

Kivligham (1997) found that group therapists who were more task oriented at the beginning of therapy and more relationship oriented at the end achieved a significant decrease in mean group distress in target problem areas.

Inevitably in a new psychodynamic psychotherapy group, someone in the group will share a problem or conflict, and the group members will try to solve it through suggestions. You might wish to suggest alternatives which might be helpful, such as mutual disclosure or sharing of feelings about the other member. You may also want to introduce the concept of group process or how the group is functioning, at the beginning. For example, if the group is ignoring a concern or feeling brought up by another member, you might point this out; you can ask the group members both to explore their feelings about ignoring that group member's disclosure and to understand why this has happened.

At the beginning stages or in the early sessions of a new psychodynamic group, the members must learn how to be effective group members. It is up to you to help the group develop norms for group functioning. Norms are behavioral rules which will direct the development of and interaction between members of the group. Norms are developed from explicit and implicit directions from you, the leader. It is inevitable that group members will spend too much time talking about outside problems, often seeking advice for quick fixes, asking too many questions, failing to address group processes. Through being a model and technical expert, you, as the group leader, must develop norms which lead to a productive psychodynamic group experience.

When a new member enters an established psychodynamic group, the group must deal with:

1. initiation rites: these can come in the form of questions about why the person is there, bragging about the specialness of the group, excluding the new member by telling experiences which are not pertinent to group growth, and reminiscing
2. expressed concerns that a new member will slow up the group
3. trust issues
4. confidentiality issues
5. jealousy of the new member's being protected by the leader
6. envisioning the new member as a rival
7. threat to the group's cohesiveness

As the group leader, look for the above issues. They might be disguised in the group and spoken about indirectly. For example, a group member might start talking about how his younger brother was given preferential treatment in the family. You, as the group leader, might consider exploring with the group if they were jealous or concerned about the new member's coming into group.

Or a group member might start to talk about people who had come and gone in this group. You might consider asking if that group member is missing the old group as it was structured, or you might point out to the group that she is excluding the new member.

ECLECTIC GROUPS

The new group: After you have brought the clients into the group room and they have been seated, after a few minutes of chatting, you can start with an exploration of how people are feeling—rather than opening the session in a more formal way with introductions. The introductions can come later in this first session.

As a reminder, the contract has been established with each client individually. Regarding silence, you have already said that the responsibility for working in group is each individual client's. Hence, after a period of silence, you might remind them of this. Should the silence continue, ask them how they feel about the silence and what each group member is experiencing.

If there is a prior acquaintanceship between members of the group, you must explore whether these members can enter into a new aspect of their relationship, observing the rule of confidentiality. That is, are they willing to engage in a new level of intimacy. If not, tell them that you will put one of them in another of your groups, asking for one of them to volunteer to do so. Should you not have another group at the time, again you could ask for one of them to volunteer not to go into the group at this time. Or you could have them "draw straws."

When bringing a new client into an existing group, you will want to make an advance announcement to the group. Tell the group a week or two in advance that a new member is joining group on such-and-such a date.

In the event that an established group member has a prior acquaintanceship with the new member, the established member has squatter's rights—that is, the established member has first choice regarding whether he or she is willing to engage in a new level of intimacy with the potential new member. If the established member chooses not to, you can place the new member in another group. If the established member doesn't have a problem with the new member's joining the group, it's the new member's choice regarding joining this group. Again, if unwilling, the new member would join another group or continue in individual therapy for a time.

In discussing with new clients the possibility of joining a group, you may encourage the clients to make it easy on themselves as to how they get started in the group. That is, they may choose to be observers and get to know the group members before actively participating, or they may elect to begin participating in the first session. Generally speaking, new clients elect to remain observers until they develop sufficient trust to begin participating.

When the group size dwindles to three members, you may experience difficulty in keeping the group going. When the membership gets small, the group interaction can get sparse, and group members may lose interest. This could result in a mass exodus. Ideally, you will have been marketing the idea of joining the group to other of your individual clients. You may also wish to actively solicit referrals from other colleagues. You may also consider changing the time and/or the day that the group meets in order to accommodate the needs of new members.

REFERENCE

Kivlighan, D. M. & Lilly, R. L. (1997). Developmental changes in group climate as they relate to therapeutic gain. *Group Dynamics: Theory, Research, and Practice, 1,* 208–221.

Cotherapy

EMANUEL SHAPIRO

A colleague and I formed a group from both our practices. I found my partner's interventions disturbing. When I approached her, she convinced me that I should tolerate her differences as she did mine. After a month, my patients told me, "Keep that woman away from me!" They experienced her as imposing interpretations without hearing the members.

I attempted to discuss this with my cotherapist to no avail. She was leading the way she knew how to lead, and her patients seemed to respond well. As a result of the unresolved tensions, the group was dissolved.

The moral is "Choose your cotherapist as carefully as you would your mate."

This chapter will discuss cotherapy—the shared leadership of a therapy group. There are several valid reasons for creating a cotherapy relationship. This relationship, which has many of the characteristics of a marriage, requires a good match of partners. The following discourse will present the views of several leading theorists detailing the positives and negatives of cotherapy for the therapist as well as the patient and the factors involved in the choice of a co-leader.

Cotherapy is not a new practice. In the 1920s, Adler (1930) first experimented using two counselors instead of one to break through resistances in children. The first psychotherapy group in a U.S. hospital was co-led by Schilder and Shaskan in 1936 (Shaskan & Roller, 1985). As far back as 1909, Moreno used individuals to represent the Director, the Alter-Ego, and the Audience, in essence, a use of cotherapists (Rosenbaum, 1978).

Roller and Nelson (1991) define cotherapy as a special practice of psychotherapy in which two therapists treat a patient or patients in any mode of treatment at the same place at the same time. Their approach emphasizes cotherapy as a special practice of psychotherapy in which the relationship between the therapists is fundamental to the treatment process. "Cotherapy is a relationship in which two therapists embody and model, both verbally and non-verbally, emotional congruence, high self-esteem, and clear and direct communication" (Roller & Nelson, 1991, p. 3).

Roller and Nelson (1991) maintain cotherapy is a form of treatment in and of itself. It is a practice of psychotherapy that possesses its own unique set of techniques. It is a form of treatment in which the relationship between the cotherapists becomes a crucial factor in both the healing and change processes. It is not a technique which would imply an operation that can be applied and then discarded. They view the relationship between cotherapists as similar to the relationship between parents who desire to coparent their children in equal fashion.

To a great extent, the use of cotherapists originally came into being as a shortcut for the training of group therapists (Rosenbaum, 1978). Soon, however, the similarity to the family structure became apparent and the idea of reproducing the family structure, with two parents, became a therapeutic plan. Roller and Nelson (1991) believe that both the supervisor-trainee and trainee-trainee teams do not constitute true cotherapy. The first, because it is not an equal relationship and the latter, because neither is a full-fledged therapist.

To avoid the pitfalls of unequal or novice leaders, Rutan and Alonso (1980) experimented with sequential cotherapy, a format where the leaders each led the group alternately for 10 sessions while the other sat silently in the group. This met the training needs of students as well as the clinical needs of patients. The leaders shared responsibility for running the group, but only one leader was immediately responsible on his or her own while leading the group. This avoids the difficulties that occur when two therapists of unequal ability or equal inexperience lead a group at the same time. In this situation, the relationship between cotherapists does not become a focus of concern. However, many of the benefits of a good cotherapy relationship are lost.

Lundin and Aronov (1951), working with groups of schizophrenics, determined that the most outstanding factor of cotherapy is the simulated family setting created by the presence of two authority figures. They caution that there must be a correct matching of the cotherapists; one should be aggressive and masculine and the other protective and feminine. They do not have to be of opposite sexes. It may be that one leader unconsciously becomes more probing or more gentle to complement his or her partner.

Besides the special advantages of role-taking, the cotherapy situation (1) may enable one therapist to supplement and/or complement the resources of the other, (2) may be easier for the two therapists to sustain group hostility so intense that it might be difficult for one therapist to bear, and (3) may allow blind spots in one therapist to be counteracted by the other's insight and perceptions.

Lundin and Aronov (1951) see the following advantages in cotherapy:

1. It provides a singular learning experience for the novice therapist.
2. The therapists can be more objective in evaluating responses of both the patients and each other at times when a leader is not actively engaged.
3. Two therapists tend to offer a broader dynamic area to which the group can react.
4. More patients can be treated in the same group.

Roller and Nelson (1991) see the following benefits of cotherapy:

1. Cotherapists can aid each other in avoiding countertransference issues. Much depends on the partners' maturity and ability to communicate.
2. Two therapists are less likely to be manipulated by a patient or group.
3. Two observers contribute to greater objectivity.
4. Patients learn about relationships as they observe two equals in power and self-esteem and model behavior as individuals in a relationship.
5. Patients have opportunities to reveal differing aspects of themselves as they relate differently to each therapist.
6. Cotherapists model different behaviors for a patient to follow. A patient can see that there is more than one right choice to the same stimulus.
7. Patients can see two persons forge a relationship over time.
8. "Cotherapy softens the tyranny of one…. A co-therapist can correct misperceptions by his or her partner and counterbalance his or her excesses" (Roller & Nelson, 1991, p. 20).
9. Role and treatment flexibility should exist between cotherapists. One therapist can be active while the other observes and evaluates. They may then alternate roles. Attention to the individual can be maintained while the cotherapist watches the group process.
10. Cotherapy permits synergy to develop. One + one is more than two.
11. Cotherapists amplify the impact of treatment in a manner not possible with an individual therapist. A cotherapy team through modeling "teaches by example the exquisite crafting of human relationships" (Roller & Nelson, 1991, p. 21).
12. Disagreement can be openly acknowledged and not threaten the standing of either partner nor will it lessen the attention to patients.

While Roller and Nelson (1991) deal with leaders of any gender combination, others consider a male and female combination essential. This combination creates a family structure that can prove quite useful. Mintz (1963) noted that the difficulty of relating to either a male or female authority figure can be worked through by patients who would have been unwilling to choose a therapist of the more threatening gender. She states that, "Cotherapy groups led jointly by a man and a woman therapist seem logical in view of the wide agreement that a basic value of group therapy is that the patient can experience and work through multiple transferences; indeed many writers believe also that another basic value of the group is its resemblance to the family" (Mintz, 1963, p. 34).

She further notes that cotherapy has been used as a deliberate technique to solve a particular problem or to reach a limited goal. In these instances, each therapist takes on a role, e.g., one behaves authoritatively and represents the superego, and the other represents the ego's integrating function. This, however, may lead to unnecessary difficulties in dealing with transference if both therapists are of the same gender.

Hulse, Ludlow, William, Rindsberg, and Epstein (1956) also advocate male and female co-leaders to facilitate the reproduction of earlier conflicts within the family. Their cotherapy experience seemed to indicate that the feelings of group members toward their own fathers and mothers could readily be observed and interpreted because of the double leadership of the group. Similarly, Markowitz and Kadis (1972), working with couples in a group, conclude that "a group structure which includes both a male and female representative of the parents is highly productive in eliciting and altering fixed transferential patterns" (p. 480).

Markowitz and Kadis (1972) describe common countertransferential attitudes in the male–female cotherapy situation:

• Overidentifying with the patient as a victim of his or her parents and covert support of destructive behavior toward them
   Example: "They deserve the way you feel about them."
• Competing with the parents to be a better parent than they were
   Example: "I alone will make you happy."
• Identifying the patient as a hated younger sibling, plus reaction formation
   Example: "You poor fellow, you are so small and weak, I must not hurt you. If I take good care of you, I will be mother's favorite son ... or my supervisor's favorite supervisee."
• Seducing the patient to act out against the commonly hated authority figure in the cotherapy setting
• Needing to be liked and favored by the patients and competing with the cotherapist, by being either overtly deprecating or covertly undermining
• Persistently missing opportunities to intercede actively in support of the cotherapist when under attack by the patients
• Being persistently impelled to help, rather than to let the patients help themselves; that is, seductively offering omnipotence and encouraging attachment rather than a separation experience
• Detaching oneself and failing to perceive what is going on.

The fact that countertransference exists between group leaders does not mean that therapists should reject cotherapy. Rather, *cotherapy countertrans-*

ference may be used to better understand the transferences in the group. For example, Kadis and Markowitz (1973) describe how a countertransference problem between the therapists was reflected in a lack of movement of the group. The two therapists ventilated their feelings about each other and their perceptions of the effect of their struggle on the group. The ability of the cotherapists to face their own feelings toward each other and to examine them helped expose the transference resistances that interfered with group progress.

Weinstein (1971) describes three basic elements of a relationship that must exist between cotherapists in order for that treatment to be effective:

- Trust
  Explanation: Does one trust one's cotherapist? Trust is defined as the belief that a cotherapist will be constructive in his or her comments and will behave appropriately toward his or her counterpart. Mistakes are not punished, but accepted and explored. Exploration of each other's dynamics as they may affect the therapy can be done in front of the patients when there is no fear regarding the relationship between the cotherapists.
- Understanding and accepting personality differences between cotherapists.
  Explanation: Each therapist, in order to best utilize his or her own abilities and talents and those of his or her cotherapist, must honestly explore his or her own strengths and weaknesses, both as a therapist and as a person. Each leader should share some of his or her self-knowledge with his or her partner so that they may work as a team. "When understanding combines with trust, each therapist is free to experiment with new techniques and ways of feeling and behaving that he has observed in his cotherapist without fear of having his 'real self' exposed or his competency threatened" (Weinstein, 1971, p. 302).
- Equal ability
  Explanation: The third necessity for successful cotherapy is the belief on the part of each leader that his or her cotherapist has equal therapeutic ability. The training situation affords a large degree of experiential difference; nevertheless, "even when a student and teacher team up, the same criteria of trust and understanding must exist as when two co-therapists of the same experience level work together" (Weinstein, 1971, p. 302). Supervisor and supervisee must openly discuss the awkwardness of their different experience levels, talents, and liabilities. Once this is accomplished, therapy may move along as quickly as when two therapists of similar experience work together. The atmosphere of mutual confidence frees both therapists to present differing perspectives.

According to Weinstein (1971), it helps if the two therapists like each other. Ideally, they should feel genuine warmth and affection toward each other. Weinstein cautions that lack of trust will lead to difficulties in co-leadership.

Gans (1962) presents guidelines to follow before two therapists decide to work together. They must consider the following:

1. Each therapist should be aware of his or her own limitations and talents.
2. Each leader is able to acknowledge the cotherapist's strengths and not exploit his or her partner's weaknesses.
3. Each leader can resist competitive temptations to vie for a dominant position.
4. The hierarchy of active over passive and dominant over submissive has been reconciled to avoid an undercurrent of resentment.
5. Each therapist has had extensive experience in individual and group therapy. (This does not pertain to training situations.)
6. Each therapist can adjust to differences in technique and theory.

Rabin (1967) suggests that Gans' guidelines can be addressed by advanced training and personal analyses of the cotherapists. Rabin gave a 50-item questionnaire comparing regular group therapy with cotherapy. A rating scale was administered to 38 participants at the American Group Psychotherapy Association conference, January, 1966. Cotherapy was felt to lead to moderately positive therapeutic movement in general and greater effectiveness in working through, in particular. They also preferred cotherapy over regular group therapy as a sole treatment modality.

Rabin's (1967) exploratory results of his test items suggests that in cotherapy:

1. A fuller transference picture will emerge.
2. The therapist will be better able to understand the patient's transference.
3. Working through especially difficult transference reactions will be easier.
4. Countertransference will be better understood.
5. Self-understanding will be enhanced.
6. There will be less emotional demands on the therapist.
7. Less experience on the part of the therapist will be needed.
8. The therapist has more gratification and fun.
9. Certain types of patients will be easier to treat; including acting out, borderline, marital couples, oral characters, and mistrustful patients.
10. Opposite gender cotherapists offer groups a place for patients to work with anxieties toward the dreaded gender.
11. The opportunity is made available for patients of both genders to identify with a relatively healthy person of the same gender.
12. Patients will be better able to work out issues of masculinity and femininity.

Rabin further notes that the vast majority of people in the study indicated that the most important aspect of cotherapy is that there be a good relationship between cotherapists. MacLennan (1965) agrees that the relationship between cotherapists is the most important criterion to be considered.

A more recent study on cotherapy conducted by Roller and Nelson (1991) found that there were nearly twice as many beneficial statements about cotherapy as statements pointing to difficulties. They concluded that the most frequent reason given for cotherapy was the increased learning opportunity that results from discussion and collaboration with a colleague. The most favorable conditions for learning occur when only slight differences between collaborators exist. Too much similarity poses no challenge and too much difference feeds frustration and conflict. Cotherapists learn a lot from each other, particularly in the experiential realm.

The second reason most often cited for choosing cotherapy was the broadened perspective offered the therapists when each has a peer observing the same events. Having another perspective of the same phenomenon can provide for different intervention options, particularly when a therapist is at an impasse with a patient or group. Additionally, one leader can correct for emotional and perceptual bias of the other. Thus, two views of personality problems and dynamics can be garnered; the cotherapy relationship offers a broader point of view.

The third most important reason for selecting cotherapy was increased transference possibilities for patients. Early memories of family scenes can be elicited by the presence of an additional transference target. Patients often choose one therapist as mother, father, sister, or brother, without respect to the therapist's gender. Roller and Nelson (1991) conclude that conducting therapy alone before conducting cotherapy is essential. Further, the interactions and dialogue between cotherapists duplicate the internal processes of the solo therapist.

Roller and Nelson (1991) seem to agree with Rabin (1967) that there is greater therapist gratification in conducting cotherapy. Therefore, Roller and Nelson describe in detail ways in which cotherapy gratifies group therapists. A cotherapy unit is able to provide mutual appreciation for accomplishment. It also provides a barrier against burnout. Therapists may be so completely involved in the demands of their own practice that they may become isolated from the work of their colleagues. Cotherapy allows therapists to work alongside colleagues and exchange emotional support and thoughts about their work and the field. Countertransference reactions, which are frequent in the burnout syndrome, can be discussed and worked through with the aid of a cotherapist. Thus, cotherapists grow, not only professionally but personally, by their collaboration, which increases their enthusiasm for psychotherapy.

As in most things in life, there is a practical side to working with a cotherapist—shared resources. Two therapists can divide responsibilities, such as answering telephone calls and scheduling appointments. Two therapists are able to share the responsibility of forming and maintaining a group. The energy necessary to carry the burden of a group psychotherapy practice is considerable; co-leaders can share the cost, effort, and publicizing of their group. The energy and work of starting a group can be especially demanding. To ease this pressure, leaders can refer from two practices to one group. A back-up therapist helps to reduce the anxiety for each group. This situation naturally leads to coverage for the group by a professional who has both knowledge and experience with the patients. The continuity of care for the group is guaranteed if one therapist is away for any reason. A cotherapist can stop leading the group temporarily with the full knowledge that the group will continue because his or her colleague will maintain the responsibilities. This kind of shared coverage allows for continued income of an absent leader. Thus, cotherapists in private practice provide for the economic security of each other.

Cotherapists can share the difficult decisions and confrontations in psychotherapy and the consequences of inevitable mistakes. They can collaborate in major treatment decisions about when to intervene and when not to treat. Roller and Nelson (1991) also perceive that the practical realm demonstrates the benefits of complementary styles and abilities in cotherapists. For example, one may be particularly good at getting referrals, networking and, in general, marketing the team. The other cotherapist may be better at interviewing clients, enlisting their trust, and establishing a bond in the early stages of treatment.

In summary, there are many reasons to lead groups in a cotherapy format. These include replication of the two-parent family, increased transference opportunities, countertransference corrections, a broader perceptual base, therapist support, and greater therapist gratification. With proper preparation of therapists, combined with their mutual trust and respect, it can be a formidable therapeutic force.

REFERENCES

Adler, A. (1930). *Guiding the child on the principles of individual psychology.* New York: Greenberg.

Gans, R. W. (1962). Group cotherapists and the therapeutic situation: A critical evaluation. *International Journal of Group Psychotherapy, 12,* 82–88.

Hulse, W. C., Ludlow, W. V., William, V., Rindsberg, B. K., & Epstein, N. B. (1956). Transference reactions in a group of female patients to male and female co-leaders. *International Journal of Group Psychotherapy, 6,* 430–435.

Kadis, A. L., & Markowitz, M. (1973). Countertransference between cotherapists in a couples psychotherapy group. In L. R. Wolberg & E. K. Schwartz (Eds.), *Group therapy 1973: An overview* (pp. 113–120). New York: Stratton Intercontinental Medical Books.

Lundin, W. H., & Aronov, B. M. (1951). The use of cotherapists in group therapy. *Journal of Counseling Psychology, 16,* 76–80.

MacLennan, B. W. (1965). Cotherapy. *International Journal of Group Psychotherapy, 27,* 34–39.

Markowitz, M., & Kadis, A. L. (1972). Short-term analytic treatment of married couples in a group by a therapist couple. In C. J. Sager & H. S. Kaplan (Eds.), *Progress in group and family therapy* (pp. 463–482). New York: Brunner/Mazel.

Mintz, E. E. (1963). Transference in cotherapy groups. *Journal of Consulting & Clinical Psychology, 27,* 34–39.

Rabin, H. M. (1967). How does cotherapy compare with regular group therapy? *American Journal of Psychotherapy, 21,* 244–255.

Roller, B., & Nelson, V. (1991) *The art of cotherapy: How therapists work together.* New York: Guilford Press.

Rosenbaum, M. (1978). The co-therapeutic method in the psychoanalytic group. In H. Mullan & M. Rosenbaum (Eds.) *Group psychotherapy* (2nd. ed., pp. 153–173). New York: MacMillan.

Rutan, J. S., & Alonso, A. (1980). Sequential cotherapy of groups for training and clinical care. *Group, 4,* 40–50.

Shaskan, D. A. & Roller, W. L. (1985). *Paul Schilder: Mind explorer.* New York: Human Sciences Press.

Weinstein, I. P. (1971). Guidelines on the choice of a co-therapist. *Psychotherapy: Theory, research and practice, 4,* 301–303.

CHAPTER 10

Special Groups

EMANUEL SHAPIRO

Al, a 32-year-old homosexual male, worked as a school social worker. His presenting problems included anxiety, depression, and narcissistic vulnerability. He was the younger of two siblings in a middle-class Italian family residing in a suburb of New York. Of primary concern to Al was that he be able to maintain a heterosexual facade in the workplace and with his friends and family. He had a secret life wherein he met lovers in gay bars. Although his goal in treatment was to remain homosexual, he suffered great shame for his intense interest in men. His heterosexual facade was so developed that, for several months, Al found himself engaged to a woman.

Al was seen for several years in individual treatment and for two additional years in combined individual and group therapy. He experienced me as empathic, yet felt our differences pointedly. He believed that he was fully accepted as himself by the group and the therapist, but experienced a poignant sense of alienation. He experienced the other group members as sharing a bond to which he could not fully connect.

Little by little, I began to appreciate that Al needed to be with others who shared the secret part of this life. The group explored Al's need for bonding with others similar to himself in his sexual life. The group, including Al, came to a consensus that a homosexual group led by a homosexual leader might give him the sense of bonding that he missed. We all seemed to understand that Al needed to experience a greater sense of kinship in his therapy. This is not to say that Al did not have strong bonds with various members of the group and to the group as a whole. It was some basic sense of sameness, something about the shared, shameful secret and society's potential ostracism, that was lacking in this group setting.

Al shared his search for the "proper group" and the "proper group therapist" with the group. When he finally found the group for which he was searching, he slowly worked toward termination in my group. Years later, Al contacted me and gratefully acknowledged the importance of my understanding and support for his bonding needs. He stated that he was no longer in treatment, but should he seek treatment at this point in his life, he would prefer a group like his first group. If I had to do this over again, I would have placed Al first in a sexual-orientation homogeneous group and later in a heterogeneous analytic group.

There are many situations which call for a "special group"—a group designed for a specific situation or population. This chapter will discuss the contributions of several authors on the various types of special groups. Their views of the group leader's role in working with such groups and the pros and cons of forming these groups will be explored.

Basically, there are five applications of the group method: personal growth, training for professionals, resolving intragroup and intergroup tensions, community education, and using group as a research tool (Goldberg, 1970). However, due to different leadership styles, there are as many varieties of groups as there are group leaders. Each group leader has his or her own notions about emotional learning, psychotherapy theory, and group training. "If we allow some leeway in the practitioner's conversion of a theory to meet his or her own personality prerequisites, it becomes possible to classify sensitivity training groups into a number of distinct … categories" (Goldberg, 1970, pp. 37–38). Thus, Goldberg systematized all treatment, interpersonal learning and training groups into 12 different divisions: Bion, psychodrama, marathon, Gestalt, encounter, basic encounter, T-group, Esalen and human potentials, interpersonal skills, discussion, self-analytic, and process group. Currently, therapy groups and training groups are the most usual leader-directed groups. In addition, there are self-help groups, which have flourished in recent years.

The basic difference between a training and a therapy group involves the function of the leader, the tasks of the participants, group composition, and, most importantly, the goals and emphasis of the two groups (Leopold, 1973). While the therapeutic aims for patients in group or individual treatment range from symptom removal to intrapsychic reorganization and reconstruction, the primary goal in a training group is centered on the group. In the training situation, group formation, group roles, and group behavior are the significant parameters. The participant's manner of relating and his or her contribution to the group are of primary concern, not personal or emotional change. Modification of the group member's behavior is a side effect in the pursuit of this sole objective, namely, "groupness" (Leopold, 1973).

The training group is a modality in its own right; it has external, task-oriented goals and is time-limited. It uses the group as a medium to educate the trainee in group dynamics. Thus, if there is personal growth, it results from the participant's self-awareness through interaction with others. Learning takes place on an experiential level by placing the responsibility for full participation on its members (Leopold, 1973).

In a therapy group, the leader sets the time and length of the group meetings. In a training or process group, the administration sets these parameters. A therapy group runs for an indeterminate number of sessions, with members leaving as they improve. A process group's existence is usually limited by the completion of a training program. In a therapy group, the therapist selects the patients to be in a group. In a training group, membership is often determined by who is in the training program. In a psychotherapy group, there is usually a rule or principle forbidding socialization, while, in the process group, the members must work and/or take classes together. This leads to subgrouping as a natural outgrowth of the student's work or relationships. In contrast, subgrouping is considered as a resistance in a therapy group.

A further difference between training and therapy groups is the students' reluctance to self-disclose in a training group (Swiller, Lang, & Halperin, 1993). The reality is that the students in training groups have ongoing collegial and competitive relationships. The issue of what makes for appropriate self-disclosure often becomes an ongoing theme in a training group. This results in complicating the contract the leader has with the group by involving a third party, the administration. For effective group functioning, the administration has to agree that the leader will provide no evaluations of the work, talents, or limitations of specific members. The contract includes the leader's agreement to help the group study its own behavior. The leader promises confidentiality and often commits to having no administrative role. The group members agree to participate in the work of the group—the study of the group's behavior. Obstacles to this arise in the form of unconscious erotic, dependent, and aggressive feelings. The group studies these feelings and the defensive responses to them. Then, the specific mechanics of these resistances are explored in the here and now. However, the training group leader should not be influenced by therapeutic considerations. The leader's job is to enable the group to learn the essence of group dynamics (Swiller *et al.*, 1993).

The leader helps the training group investigate its boundaries, including the time and place of meetings and the composition at each meeting. The leader must function as a "gatekeeper" of the boundaries, by ensuring the room is ready and starting the group at the appropriate time. Leopold (1973) suggests that, in the first few sessions, the leader should be nondirective and even passive, in order to allow a group in its early stage to establish its own identity as a unit. Later, he or she may have to function as a catalyst. Swiller *et al.* (1993), on the other hand, believe that the leader should be active at the beginning, but as the group matures, more and more of the work should be done by the members themselves. At times, in response to the stresses that impact upon the group, the leader may encourage supportive-ness and nurturing between the members and not focus on learning. At other times, he or she may intervene to point out group dynamics or behavioral attitudes and roles of the individual which affect the group's functioning. The learning experience in training groups is particularly valuable for those members who desire to assume leadership roles in professional or training situations.

Training groups focus on the nature of group process. Goldberg (1970) points out that group process has to do with what makes a group, how it functions to develop and maintain its group quality, and what effects it has on its members. "Group process includes all those acts, behaviors, thoughts, and feelings, both overt and covert, that are activated when a group of people come together and are aware of one another's presence" (Goldberg, 1970, p. 223). The word "process" is used to emphasize that behaviors in a group are not discrete units that are unrelated to previous experiences in the group. All group activities that are involved in group process are related and influence the future course of the group's actions. Group process, therefore, has direction and continuity. Further-more, if the underlying disturbances in a group can be determined, the relation-ship between observed actions and unconscious material can be easily addressed. "Group process includes the ways in which group members inter-change feelings, thoughts, and values, and the precise types of relationships and activities that result from these interchanges" (Goldberg, 1970, p. 224). From this view, the behavior of any member of the group cannot be comprehended unless attention is first given to what is happening to the group as a whole.

The faculty of the American Group Psychotherapy Association meetings often find themselves leading institute groups for AGPA or workshop groups for group training programs. These are time-limited groups with four or five sessions over a two- or three-day period. Often, they are meant to demonstrate analytic or psychodynamic principles via the experiences of the members. They differ somewhat from an ongoing process group. Institute or workshop groups are often a blend of a training group and an analytic group. They have the boundary issues of the process group, but more attention is paid to indi-vidual dynamics. Yalom (1985) states that the adaptation of analytic group therapy can be made to specialized situations.

Yalom (1985) believes that, before dealing with special kinds of groups, the leader should first master fundamental group therapy theory and then obtain a deep understanding of the primal prototypic therapy group:

But which group therapy represents the most archaic common ancestor? There has been such a luxuriant growth of group therapies that it requires great perspicacity to find, amidst the thicket, the primal trunk of group therapy. But if there is a primal or ancestral group therapy ... it was the first group therapy; it remains the most deeply studied ... furthermore, it has stimulated ... an imposing body of professional literature containing the observations and conclusions of thoughtful clinicians (p. 457).

Yalom recommends that one follow three steps when developing a specialized therapy group:

1. Evaluate the clinical setting in order to determine the unalterable variables.
2. Set goals that are appropriate and feasible within the existing limitations.
3. Alter the classical technique while retaining the basic concepts and therapeutic factors of psychodynamic group therapy, but modify techniques to adapt to the new setting in order to achieve the delineated goals.

Group psychotherapists have added to their repertoire the treatment of people in groups who share a similar life-condition or clinical disorder. Certain therapeutic advantages account for the expansion of these homogeneous groups. The benefits include the therapeutic gains derived from a shared condition. Yalom (1985) suggests that such groups "jell" more quickly and offer instantaneous support. In contrast to heterogeneous groups, homogeneous groups provide "a more immediate source of identification and understanding, a clearer sense of group purpose, and increased cohesiveness. Other reported benefits of homogeneous groups include a shortened period of treatment, less resistance, fewer cliques, better attendance, and a quicker symptomatic relief." (Seligman & Marshak, 1990, p. v).

Homogeneous groups tend to have the following characteristics:

1. They are session limited.
2. They are closed to additional members.
3. They relate to a specific, defined issue.
4. They are strongly goal-oriented.
5. They have a high degree of structure.
6. They have a high educational function.
7. They discourage attention to transference issues.

For many group therapists, the downside of a homogeneous group is that it tends to remain at a more superficial level than does the heterogeneous, psychodynamic group and "is an ineffective medium for the altering of character structure" (Yalom, 1985, p. 265). To address this concern, many clinicians will have time-limited groups, such as survivors of rape or incest, that will result in some clients becoming patients in ongoing psychodynamic groups.

One very popular type of homogeneous group is the self-help group; the most familiar of these is Alcoholics Anonymous. Lieberman (1990) has attempted to find a place for the trained group therapist in the world of self-help groups. He states that such groups are highly prevalent and increasing rapidly. Results from a recent national survey reported findings on 1-year utilization rates from a national sample of over 3000 households are as follows: 5.6% sought mental health professionals, 5% sought clergy, and 5.8% used self-help groups. "These findings suggest that mutual aid groups are a major and growing source of therapeutic treatment for a variety of physical and emotional difficulties, and estimates that 12 to 14 million adult Americans utilize such groups..." (Lieberman, 1990, p. 3). The range of issues and problems that concern self-help groups is broad and appears to be increasing geometrically. "Almost any definable physical and emotional problem, as well as stigmatized conditions and feelings of deviance, provides an opportunity for the formation of such groups" (Lieberman, 1990, p. 3).

Lieberman raises the question of whether or not the spread of self-help groups that are similar to, but not identical with, psychotherapy groups poses a problem for professionals. Superficially, the answer seems to be an obvious yes. However, research has demonstrated that over 25% of the participants in self-help groups for widows and widowers utilized professional psychotherapeutic services, while only 4% of the general population, not in self-help groups, availed themselves of such services (Lieberman, 1990). These results imply that self-help groups may serve as preparation for entry into therapy groups.

Yalom (1985) theorized that group principles may be applied to specialized groups, but he was dealing only with professionally led groups. Thus, self-help groups, by definition leaderless, cannot be put in the same category. Lieberman (1990) states that the transfer of group therapy methods to self-help groups by leaders educated in the helping-profession methodology is not a productive use of a therapist's expertise. There are fundamental differences between group psychotherapy and the self-help group model. First is the emphasis by group therapists on therapeutic strategies that were based on the perception of the group as a social microcosm. Second, therapists have intervention styles that are based upon a highly complex system of techniques. Third, and most important, therapists believe that personal growth is based on reworking relationships in the group. All three are not characteristic of self-help groups, nor are they strategies that would be appropriately employed by nonprofessionals. This disparity cannot be remedied by the training of group leaders in professional techniques. That would serve to increase the psychological distance between the group leader and the rest of the members. Relationships in a self-help group are relationships between equals. Professionals need to recognize that self-help groups engage in a fundamentally different activity for dealing with emotional distress and behavior problems from the treatment provided by clinically trained group therapists. Self-help groups are highly specific institutions with their own customs and traditions; these are what make them successful. They have developed a complex ideology out of the experiences of the members themselves. It is important for professionals to be aware that it is a set of shared values which enables most self-help groups to develop and maintain themselves. Professionals must be sensitive to those ideas which address the cause and treatment of problems. "These ideas may often be diametrically opposed to a professional view of the nature of the problem and most particularly the procedures for helping" (Lieberman, 1990, p. 15).

There is a place for professionals, according to Lieberman (1990). Group psychotherapists should consult with self-help groups and not attempt to treat them. Group therapists have training and tools that enable them to bring together a group of individuals and create a working social system in which they use their therapeutic abilities. The therapist can use these skills to advise self-help groups and to manage problem situations, such as high turnover and membership nonparticipation. Often, new self-help groups borrow the ideology and methodology of successful self-help groups. The group therapist can help in this adaptation by clarifying which aspects of the successful group would be valuable to the new group. Lieberman (1990) believes that a critical function of the group therapist is to aid in the legitimization of such groups. He suggests that referrals to self-help groups and the provision of consultative support for referrals from self-help groups will serve this purpose.

In summary, there is an extensive variety of groups that range from professionally led therapy groups to leaderless self-help groups. Leadership functions vary with the goals and type of group. In adapting a psychodynamic group to a population with special needs, the therapist must maintain basic group concepts and adjust them appropriately to the immutable restraints of the new situation. The group therapist's relationship to self-help groups should be consultative and supportive, without attempting to impose psychodynamic theory onto the values and processes of self-help groups.

REFERENCES

Goldberg, C. (1970). *Encounter: Group sensitivity training experience* (pp. 37–61). New York: Science House.

Leopold, H. S. (1973). Beyond the traditional therapy group. In L. R. Wolberg & E. K. Schwartz (Eds.), *Group therapy 1973: An overview* (pp. 121–128). New York: Intercontinental Medical Book Corp.

Lieberman, M. (1990). A group therapist perspective on self-help groups. In M. Seligman & L. E. Marshak (Eds.), *Group psychotherapy: Interventions with special populations* (pp. 1–17). Needham Heights, MA: Simon & Schuster.

Seligman, M., & Marshak, L. E. (1990). Preface. In M. Seligman & L. E. Marshak (Eds.), *Group psychotherapy: Interventions with special populations* (pp. v-vi). Needham Heights, MA: Simon & Schuster.

Swiller, H. I., Lang, E. A., & Halperin, D. A. (1993). Process groups for training. In A. Alonso & H. I. Swiller (Eds.), *Psychotherapy residents in group therapy in clinical practice* (pp. 533–545). Washington: American Psychiatric Press.

Yalom, I. D. (1985). *The theory and practice of group psychotherapy* (4th ed.). New York: Basic Books.

CHAPTER 11

Reprise: Some Guidelines for Group Therapists*

J. Scott Rutan and Anne Alonso

People talk about things in group that, in no way, would they talk about otherwise. One young man talked about some very mild sexual touching of his younger sister, years earlier, when she was 3 years old. He was having trouble forgiving himself.

Several others opened up about similar experiences. They said they could never have talked about their own experiences had he not talked about his. People can learn to forgive themselves through revealing their secrets.

Psychodynamic group psychotherapy works on the basis of two major premises: (1) Individuals will present themselves, complete with strengths and weaknesses, in a group in fundamentally the same ways as they live out their lives; and (2) the various behaviors that occur within groups are interconnected via group associations and group contagion.

A brief example will serve to illustrate both points. Let us suppose a group of eight strangers is meeting for the first time. All eight individuals will adopt their own characteristic styles for coping with that situation. One may boisterously assume dominance by helping with introductions, acting as chairperson, and generally presenting a self-confident image. Another individual may sit mutely throughout the meeting. Still another member may demonstrate and speak of the anxiety of the situation. Yet another may plead or demand that the leader assume more responsibility for the meeting.

In other words, from the very moment they enter the group room, individuals will begin to demonstrate their characteristic styles for coping and living.

* Reprinted with permission from Rutan, J. Scott & Alonso, Anne (1994). Reprise: some guidelines for group therapists. *Group.* 18(1), 56–63.

One may presume that the initial meeting of a therapy group presents each member with a fairly constant stimulus. The situation evokes for everyone, including leaders, issues of basic trust. Will this be a safe situation? Will I be treated with respect or abuse? How can the blind lead the blind? Will there be enough time and attention for me? What can I do to protect myself and to gain something for myself? Do I dare risk allowing others and myself to know what I feel?

The individuals cited above indicated their first-line defenses against these concerns. We noted a counterphobic refusal to acknowledge the fear, or, at least, an attempt to master it by active assertiveness; we saw a regression to a mute, totally passive position; we noted one member acknowledged the anxiety verbally and behaviorally; and we noted one member who demonstrated a pervasive dependency and entitlement that implied it was the responsibility of the leader to remove the anxiety. From the moment the group begins, the patients not only talk about their problems, they have them, not just in the transference but in the real interactions within the minicommunity. We may assume that the styles presented by individuals in groups are not newly developed for just this situation, but rather, that we are privy to observing styles that have been historically utilized by these individuals.

The role of the group therapist is to help our patients understand themselves by understanding their interactions in their therapy group. And a major problem that confronts group therapists, perhaps uniquely, is the difficult task of selecting the most useful data from the massive amount of data that is generated by a therapy group. As the therapist observes the continuing and continual interactions of individuals in a group, how does he or she determine what is most salient and useful?

Little has been written to assist the group therapist in discriminating the importance of material presented in each group meeting. A major reason why there is a paucity of literature on this matter is that the process of a therapy group is entirely too unpredictable to allow for stereotypic "rules" for leaders to follow. Nonetheless, it seems to the authors that there are some overall guidelines that can inform therapists as to how to evaluate data that are presented in groups. These guidelines are particularly geared toward helping therapists become more aware of the ongoing process issues occurring in group meetings.

GUIDELINES

Build Hypotheses

One historically validated method of determining "causative" data and separating them from irrelevant data has been hypothesis testing. While it is true that the social sciences do not allow the controls necessary for complete hypothesis testing and an ongoing group is not a rigorously controlled situation, nonetheless, the leader can begin developing hypotheses and examining the group data in light of those hypotheses.

For example, most therapists will review their notes from a previous group meeting prior to beginning a session. The implication of such an act is that the present meeting may continue some themes that were begun the week before. If the therapist allows himself or herself to become more rigorous about the task of generating hypotheses, the flood of data in group meetings may take on more immediate relevance.

> **Case Example 1**   The week before, the therapist had announced to his group that a new member, sex not mentioned, would be joining the group. However, during the week, the new patient had notified the therapist that he had changed his mind and would not be joining. In the previous meeting, the group, a rather new group, had denied the importance of a new member's joining, though the therapist felt that a new member would have powerful impact. Beyond the typical issues involved in a new member's joining, the members of this group had experienced several dropouts and were feeling that the group would fail and that they would be left on their own. The announcement of a new member was the first demonstration of a visible sort that the leader, a psychiatric resident, intended to continue the group.
>
> Prior to entering the current meeting, the therapist and his supervisor began generating hypotheses as to how the group members would respond to the knowledge that the new member would not be coming, after all.
>
> It was presumed, for example, that one woman would associate to feelings about a pregnancy that had resulted in a dead baby; that a young man would associate to his father's repeated promises to come and rescue him from Mother—promises never kept.
>
> It was further hypothesized that the group as a whole would overtly express very little reaction to the new member's not joining, but that covertly the reactions would be strong and would pervade the meeting.
>
> The leader opened the meeting with his announcement and then said nothing for the next 45 minutes. In this instance, the hypotheses proved apt. The members made very little comment about the new member's not joining, with a theme being, "Good, we'll not have to put up with meeting a stranger."
>
> However, the process of the meeting moved quickly to anger and unkept promises, fathers not strong enough to deliver the goods, and then to sadness and mourning, including some material about members feeling unlovable.
>
> The woman mentioned above suddenly fell silent about 15 minutes into the meeting, then began weeping, and finally said she was filled with renewed grief over the child she had so yearned for, which was born dead. The man mentioned above was furious with the leader, without any conscious connection to the new member's not joining or to his own father. Some weeks later, the young man made the connections and did some profitable work on his distrust of the leader and of "fathers" in general.

By virtue of making some educated guesses in advance of the meeting, the therapist was able to look at the group material from a particularly helpful perspective. This "head start" enabled him to follow the associations and not be overwhelmed by the flood of data.

Hypothesis testing may be used in a variety of ways. The example given above concerns hypothesizing about the process of a given meeting. It is equally possible to hypothesize about the reactions of specific patients to specific situations (e.g., vacations, terminations of other members, holiday seasons, etc.). The added benefit of the use of hypotheses is that if they bear out, the therapist has some confirmation that he or she is on the right track.

There is a danger in hypothesis-generating, of course. It is possible for a therapist to become dedicated to his or her hypothesis and thereby overlook new or more important data. But if a therapist can let go of an hypothesis that is either erroneous or not currently relevant, then the generating of hypotheses can be a particularly valuable means of sorting out the group data.

Take Your Time

One of the most important safeguards against countertransference error is the passage of time. The authors often suggest to our supervisees that they sit silently for the first half-hour of their group meetings. The primary purpose of this exercise is not to frustrate the group and thus to promote affect, though this often occurs as well. Rather, it is to allow the leader time to begin to see the patterns developing in a particular meeting.

> **Case Example 2**   A group began with various members asking questions of the leader. The questions ranged from "Will you be taking a vacation this year?" to "Will you increase my medication?" The leader could not see a connecting thread to the early part of the meeting, except that members were attempting to engage him directly. He did not respond to the questions, and the group went on to angry feelings about his not giving enough.
>
> Eventually, however, the members began confronting a particularly volatile member of the group. The confrontation had been brewing for a number of weeks, but the members were frightened of the potential response of the particular member in question. As the affect got more and more heated, the members began looking to the leader for assistance and protection.
>
> By virtue of not having intervened too quickly, the leader had allowed the group to get to the material that was the most important agenda. Further, he had allowed himself and the group to understand more fully the behaviors that began the group. In light of what followed, it became clear that the members were needful of knowing that the leader was available, and just how available, before they began to deal overtly with their anger at a particularly frightening fellow member.
>
> The leader was able to help the members understand this process and was also able to assist them to associate back to the yearning for protection by parents that was keenly important to the development of these patients.

Too often, we as group therapists get sidetracked by responding too quickly. If we take our time, the themes of a particular meeting often begin to take much clearer shape.

There is a wide variety of explanations for this tendency to jump in too quickly. Countertransference certainly accounts for a great deal of therapist impatience. We have been struck by how often "interpretation" is used as a defense by the therapist. That is, a therapist will offer a premature interpretation primarily (though unconsciously) as a means of diluting the affect that is beginning to build. Another countertransference trap that leads to impatience in the therapist is the misguided notion that we must always appear "in charge" and "in control." Often, when our patients most need to bear the ambiguities of their lives and feelings, the therapist begins to experience that same ambiguity and feels a need to demonstrate that he or she really knows what is happening. Yet another cause of therapists reacting too quickly in group is the mistaken idea that our patients cannot tolerate anxiety and deprivation for even $1^1/_2$ hours. We do feel obligated to answer a patient's question if we judge the question to be appropriate, for example. But we do not feel obligated to answer the question when it is asked! Often, we find it much more profitable to delay an answer until the patient has had the opportunity to explore the affect surrounding the question. In this way, it is sometimes determined that the question, though appropriate at a reality level, was ultimately irrelevant, and that other, much more potent, material was beneath it. That information would be missed if the question were immediately considered to be simply a question. This dynamic is continually present in groups, and patience with our patients is indeed a virtue.

Note the Beginning

A third guideline for therapists trying to sift through the mass of data that groups generate is to pay particular attention to the first behavior or words in a group. This is predicated on the notion that the very first group behavior often forecasts the group theme that will follow.

> **Case Example 3** As the group was walking in for a meeting, one patient mentioned in an aside to another patient, "God, I'm having incredible trouble with a bill I have at the local department store."
>
> This comment was not noticed by anyone except the therapist, who filed it away for future reference. The process of the meeting began to revolve around unrequited love. Various members spoke of husbands, lovers, and parents who "don't love me as much as I love them."
>
> Ultimately, the patient who had originally made the comment about her bill said, "The unrequited love that hurts me most right now is Bill." Bill was another member of the group who had missed two meetings in a row. Clearly, she was having trouble with her "bills," and as the meeting progressed, the leader and the patient were able to see together how her unconscious was forecasting the feelings that would eventually come to the surface for her.

The focusing on the first behavior in a meeting can reduce itself to "gimmickry" if it is used injudiciously. However, the simple filing away of that first behavior by the therapist, for future reference, if relevant, can often be very useful in providing some framework for understanding the flow of material in a given meeting. Typically, the behavior, if relevant at all, is "coded," as shown in the previous example. If the beginning of the group behavior is more overt, the group simply picks it up and begins work right there. Another example of the more coded information would be the new male patient who walked into his first meeting, cigarette in hand, and asked, "Does anyone have a match?" In the following weeks, he clearly demonstrated that his sole purpose in coming to group was just that—"to find a match," preferably a good-looking young woman of about 25.

Think Analogies

Another guideline for group therapists is to be aware of analogies. Any dynamically oriented therapist is well aware of the importance of listening for the covert, as well as the manifest, meaning of verbal content from our patients. Further, it is clear that the overt content often is analogous to the deeper, more hidden content. In group therapy, analogous or symbolic material is often presented as a defense against experiencing or presenting material that has specific reference to the group itself. Members of groups are always aware of the presence of their fellow members and are always responding to them. Very often, material that seems to have no direct connection to the life of the group itself will have, upon closer inspection, direct significance for in-group issues.

> **Case Example 4** The meeting after a group member had terminated angrily and prematurely, the group began with one member's talking about what terrible treatment she had received from her physician when she consulted him about a fever during the week. This led to a groupwide sharing of experiences with incompetent or uncaring doctors. The therapist listened quietly for some time, waiting for the group to speak more directly of the termination. Finally, the therapist drew the connection for the group by saying, "Perhaps if this doctor had been more competent or concerned, one of your colleagues would not be gone now." The group was then able to own the displaced feelings and share their hurt and angry feelings with the therapist, eventually moving on to their rage at the member who dumped them so prematurely.
>
> Particularly at those times when the group seems aimless and the leader is having difficulty understanding just what is happening, it is useful to ask oneself, "How can I understand what is presently happening as a communication about what people are feeling in this group?"

Observe Your Own Affective States

The humanity of the therapist is not discontinuous from the humanity of our patients. A key diagnostic tool that is available to the group therapist is the ability to use his or her own affective responses during a particular meeting. While it is presumed that group therapists are always willing to listen to their own affect, it becomes uniquely important at those times when the therapists are becoming confused by the process of a particular meeting.

> **Case Example 5** In one meeting, the therapist was unable to determine what was happening in the group. The members were talking, but nothing seemed to be happening. The themes seemed disconnected and the meeting seemed to be floundering. As the therapist began to explore her own affect, she realized she was feeling intensely sad. Her own associations took her to funerals, wakes, and important losses.
>
> With those data at hand, the therapist began listening to the group material for indications of similar affect in her patients. The content did not overtly reflect the mourning, but, ultimately, the therapist said, "It feels quite sad in here tonight." The group members quickly agreed and began following their associations.
>
> It was at this point that the group realized it was the anniversary of the death of the sister of one of the members of the group. This death, the result of a long and painful bout with cancer, had been very powerful in the life of the group, and it turned out that the entire group, leader included, had been involved in a delayed grief reaction.

The authors do not practice "therapist transparency," in the sense of sharing our feelings overtly with the group. It is our conviction that our patients gain more if we keep our own affective input to a minimum. However, in no way does this mean that we are not utilizing our affective responses continually as guidelines to help us understand what the group members are experiencing.

Keep the Presenting Problem and Family History in Mind at All Times

In the confusion that can arise when eight to ten patients are interacting at the same time, it is often very useful to have the individual presenting problems and histories of our patients to fall back upon to give us clarity and direction. Put simply, often our patients are "having" their problems right before our eyes.

> **Case Example 6** A young attorney had been a patient in group therapy for several months. One week, he requested that the therapist "give a credit line" for a couple of months. The patient explained that his work had not been going well and that he was financially burdened at the moment.
>
> The therapist recalled that the patient's presenting problem was his proclivity for becoming involved in highly dependent relationships, with the end result being that the patient felt so infantilized that he fled the relationships. The therapist also recalled that the family history of this patient had included a highly symbiotic relationship with the mother.
>
> While there are many good reasons for not extending a "credit line" to our patients, in this instance, the remembering of the specific problems that the patient

was working on helped the therapist formulate very clearly what was happening. At the end of the meeting, the therapist stated, "It seems clear that you are once again attempting to negotiate the very kind of dependent relationship you came here to be able to avoid. Perhaps we need to examine the feelings you are experiencing toward me…"

The patient was able to use this experience to gain insight into his fears of bearing the same adult responsibilities that other members of the group were having to bear.

Formulate a Summary

The final guideline that we would suggest is to begin preparing your summary statement at the beginning of the meeting. That is, from the moment the group starts, the therapist should be concerned with what kind of summary statement might be made at the end of the meeting to help the patients understand what has been happening in this session.

This, by the way, is not to imply that every group meeting should end with a proclamation from the leader. Rather, we are suggesting that the *preparation* of such a summary, whether or not it is used, will provide clarity for the leader as he or she attempts to follow the various themes that develop in any given meeting.

As with the hypothesis-building mentioned above, the inherent danger is that a leader will become so preoccupied with the summary being developed that he or she cannot see important material that is divergent with that "set." But if a therapist is willing to "let go" of the summary when it becomes apparent that it is not complete or is, in fact, in error, the very task of trying to structure the summary will keep the therapist helpfully focused on overall process issues throughout the meeting.

The question of whether or not to use a summary at the end of a meeting is, in itself, an intriguing one. We distinguish between three kinds of therapist response at the end of a group session. The first is like putting a period at the end of a sentence. This is a summary statement that pulls together what has gone on during the meeting, providing some affective and cognitive structuring to what has preceded. A summary of this sort "stops" the process to some extent, and it should be used when a meeting has generated a useful amount of affective data with insufficient cognitive structuring to help the patients integrate the experience. An example of this kind of comment would be that mentioned in Case Example 6. The young attorney had lots of affect and had presented his problem quite clearly. What he needed was for the therapist to point out what was happening so that the patient could begin to integrate it.

The second type of therapist response at the end of a group meeting could be likened to a comma in the middle of a sentence. In this circumstance, the leader decides that the meeting has produced some profitable data that bears further exploration, but that some tentative interpretations can be helpfully offered at this point. The result of this kind of ending statement is to cause a "pause" in the process, but not of the severity of the more complete and intensive interpretations offered in the "period" example above.

The final kind of leadership response to the end of a meeting is essentially to leave the meeting quite open-ended, making no summary or concluding remarks at all. This ending is typically something like, "Our time is up; I'll see you next week." The function of this ending is to enhance the prospects that the group will pick up at the same affective place the next week—that the group "sentence" will be uninterrupted from one week to the next. The leader will use this ending when he or she feels insufficient data has been generated to feed it back helpfully to the group.

Concluding Remarks

As we have sat in the midst of groups over the years and attempted to find helpful techniques to simplify the process of making sense of the rich data that are available to us, we have been struck primarily by how few techniques there are that routinely provide such assistance. We analyzed our own styles, trying to assess what we looked for and how we determined what was more valuable than something else, and we began to notice certain covert guidelines that were being used. We have tried to explicate these so that others can experiment as well.

Certainly, more rigorous attention needs to be paid to the whole problem of how group therapists can more effectively harvest the rich fields that are before us each week in our groups.

CHAPTER 12

Does Group Psychotherapy Work?*

ADDIE FUHRIMAN AND GARY M. BURLINGAME

I'm often asked if group psychotherapy works. Let me tell you about Julie. When Julie entered the group, she was 40 pounds overweight. She is a compassionate woman, nurse, mother, dutiful daughter. But hardly anyone seemed to be taking care of her. So she nurtured herself—by overeating. Peanut butter cookies in her top desk drawer, M&M's in her purse, a trip to Baskin-Robbins for a little treat after supper.

In group, Julie was not only liked but admired, respected. She learned to trust the group members and began to feel nurtured by them. While she was concerned about her weight and talked about dieting, she eventually realized that dealing with her frustration over the lack of nurturance was the primary issue. As she did so and began to feel the group nurturance, she began to shed pounds. While not ignoring what she ate, she nonetheless didn't "diet," as such. Result: she lost 40 pounds.

Does group psychotherapy work? It worked for Julie. If it works in five out of ten cases, it works.

The past teaches us that longevity of a treatment does not necessarily insure effectiveness (bloodletting). Even though the practice of group psychotherapy has existed on two continents for nearly a century in various forms, one must still ask: What is the cumulative empirical evidence regarding group psychotherapy's overall efficacy? Appraisal of the effectiveness of group psychotherapy requires one to first address another question: Effective in comparison to what? It is evident that reviewers have responded to this question in different ways over the past 45 years and that the method of addressing this question often seems to affect the answer derived.

* Reprinted with permission from Fuhriman, A., & Burlingame, G.M. (1994). Group psychotherapy: research and practice. In A. Fuhriman & G.M. Burlingame (Eds.). *Handbook of Group Psychotherapy: An Empirical and Clinical Synthesis.* New York: Wiley.

Early reviewers (Burchard, Michaels, & Kotkov, 1948; Thomas, 1943) address the question of effectiveness by independently cataloging studies, rather than making collective statements from the literature. One of the earliest reviews was Burchard and his colleagues (1948), who reviewed 15 scientifically oriented studies of group psychotherapy. They developed a seven-factor descriptive framework to handle the wide diversity of orientation, goals, techniques, and methods found across studies. This schema not only displayed the lack of uniformity in data reported across studies, but also demonstrated the difficulty in formulating general conclusions regarding group therapy. For instance, their evaluation dimension, which addressed the success of treatment, has the least amount of information of any dimension, and the data reported were so diverse that comparative statements are impossible to derive. After attesting to their belief in the value of group psychotherapy, these authors conclude that it was "extremely difficult to draw clear-cut distinctions between group 'therapy' and [sic] many endeavors to modify the behavior, personality, and character of human beings through group participation" (pp. 257–258). As will become evident, this remark seems to be prophetic when one considers subsequent reviews of group psychotherapy.

From the 1960s forward, reviews included more composite statements of overall efficacy and less individual cataloging of studies. Twenty-two extend from the early 1960s into the 1990s (Table I). While not exhaustive of all reviews published in the last three decades, these are representative of the general trends in how group psychotherapy has been viewed. Table I highlights the treatment orientation, the number of studies examined in a single review, what group treatment was compared with to determine its overall effectiveness, the population being treated, and finally, general outcome conclusions drawn from the review.

GROUP THERAPY OUTCOME IN THE 1960S

Several important characteristics illustrate the reviews of the 1960s. First, there is a great deal of diversity in the treatment orientations of the various studies, ranging from large group milieu and nondirective therapies to traditional analytic models of treatment (Table I). In addition to the traditional case studies and anecdotal reports that characterized most of the group literature in the first half of this century, there was an emergence of investigations that empirically compared group therapy with other experimental conditions, such as control groups (no-treatment conditions), group treatment alternatives, individual therapy, and combined treatment conditions (e.g., conjoint individual and group).

Nonetheless, most comparative studies reviewed in the 1960s were field studies that relied on captive populations and nonequivalent comparison groups. Specifically, comparison groups were often groups of convenience

TABLE I Group Psychotherapy Review Articles

Author	Treatment orientation	# of St.	Comparison WLC	OT	I	COM	Sample	Conclusions
Rickard (1962)	Nondirective, psychoanalytic psychodrama	22	X	X	X	X	Mixed inpatient & outpatient	Too much variability among patients, therapists, and measures for comparisons to be more than tentative. Efficacy of group remains to be empirically validated.
Pattison (1965)	Psychodrama, milieu, analytic	U					Inpatient, prison, addict, delinquent	Group activity is therapeutic using behavioral criteria, disappointing with psychometric criteria' and promising with construct criteria. Notes that the research on individual psychotherapy and small group research has yet to be effectively incorporated into group psychotherapy research.
Stotsky & Zolik (1965)	Psychodrama, round table & heterogeneous group	U	X	X	X	X	Psychotics	The results of controlled experimental studies do not offer clear support for using group therapy as an independent modality, but they do support group as an adjunctive or helpful intervention when combined with other treatments (drugs, individual, etc.)
Mann (1966)	Psychodrama, nondirective	41	X	X		X	Mixed diagnosis, adult & children, most institutionalized	Group therapy produces change in behavior, attitude, and personality regardless of orientation, method of comparison or instruments.
Anderson (1968)	Counseling groups	6	X	X		X	Primarily students	Group counseling associated with higher GPA and personality change when compared to control. No differences when compared to other treatment or combined.

(continues)

TABLE I continued

Author	Treatment orientation	Comparison							Sample	Conclusions
		# of St.	W L C	OT	I	COM			
Meltzoff & Komreich (1970)	Heterogeneous, expressive, nondirective, systematic desensitization, behavior, analytic	6	X		X	X		Hospitalized adults, adult outpatients, children	80% of adequately controlled studies reviewed showed primarily positive results with both individual and group therapy. Six studies which made direct comparisons between group and individual found equivalent outcome with a slight tendency for individual to be more effective.
Bednar & Lawlis (1971)	Heterogenous, group psychotherapy, self-help, activity, milieu, work, insight	38	X	X	X	X		Mixed inpatient & outpatient, delinquents, alcoholics, sex offenders, students	Group therapy is valuable in treating neurotics, psychotics, and character disorders. It is a two-edged sword that can facilitate client deteriotation.
Luborsky et al. (1975)	Heterogeneous	12	X		X	X		Unspecified	Most of the 13 comparisons showed no significant differences between group and individual treatment. There was a tie in nine comparisons; group was better in two comparisons and individual was better in two comparisons. One study had two comparisons.
Grunebaum (1975)	Unspecified	U			X			Heterogeneous	Only meager data exist comparing group and individual therapy and the evidence suggests that they are equally effective in most instances. Some findings suggest that benefits may be disorder specific, such as phobias better treated by individual therapy and group more effective for schizophrenic outpatients.

Study	Type of group	N				Population	Findings
Emrick (1975)	Heterogeneous	384	X	X	X	Alcoholics	Found a general trend for both individual and group to be effective in treating alcoholism.
Lieberman (1976)	Heterogeneous, psychotherapy, & personal growth groups	47	X		X	College students, adults	Group consistently produced favorable outcome over controls. Reported no outcome differences in studies that compared group with individual format. Noted that the indices used to measure outcome are relatively insensitive to the potentialities of different treatment contests, such as group and individual psychotherapy.
Parloff & Dies (1977)	Heterogeneous, psychotherapy groups	39	X	X	X	Psychoneurotic, schizophrenic, addiction, legal offenders	Group has no unique advantage over other treatments with schizophrenic patients; no firm conclusions can be drawn with psychoneuroses, and limited support for effectiveness with addicts.
Bednar & Kaul (1978)	Heterogeneous, behavioral, TA, unspecified group therapy, & encounter groups	21	X		X	College students, delinquents, prisoners, psychiatric patients	Group treatments have been more effective than no treatment, placebo, and other recognized psychological treatments.
Solomon (1983)	Psychodynamic, aversion	2	X		X	Alcoholics	Combined individual and group related to poorest outcome while individual and group as independent Tx showed equivalent outcomes.
Kanas (1986)	Heterogeneous	40	X		X	Outpatient & inpatient schizophrenics	Group therapy proved to be superior to controls in 67% of inpatient and 80% of outpatient studies with long-term therapy being the best
Kaul & Bednar (1986)	Experimental psychotherapy groups	17	X		X	Primarily adult mixed diagnosis	Mixed but favorable outcomes for the efficacy of group psychotherapy.

(continues)

TABLE I continued

Author	Treatment orientation	# of St.	Comparison					Sample	Conclusions
			W L C	OT	I	COM			
Toseland & Siporin (1986)	Heterogeneous	32	X		X		Heterogeneous	Results of this review indicated that group treatment was as effective as individual treatment in 75% of the studies included, and was more effective in 25%. In the 32 studies reviewed, there was no case in which individual treatment was found to be more effective than group treatment.
Bostwick (1987)	Unspecified	13			X	X	Unspecified	Individual treatment had less premature termination than group while combined individual and group treatment proved superior in reducing drop-outs over either modality.
Oesterheld et al. (1987)	Heterogeneous (e.g., behavioral, insight, cognitive-behavioral, dynamic)	18	X	X	X		Bulimia	Group seems to be helpful but methodological limitations preclude robust conclusions.
Zimpfer (1987)	Heterogeneous (e.g., group counseling, multi-modal, growth, insight)	19	X	X			Elderly	Group has no significant advantage over other therapies.
Freeman & Munro (1988)	Cognitive-behavioral, eclectic, supportive, didactic	13	X	X	X	X	Bulimia	Neither drug or group as effective as individual but all are more effective than placebo. Group most cost-effective and combined group and individual most effective of all treatments.

Study	Treatment type	N				Population	Conclusions
Cox & Merkel (1989)	Heterogeneous	32	X	X	X	Bulimia	In a review of 15 groups and 17 individual studies (only one study provided a comparison between the the two modalities, the rest were inferential), it was concluded that there was no support for the two treatments having any differential effectiveness.
Zimpfer (1990)	Cognitive-behavioral, psychoeducational behavior	31	X	X		Bulimia	Regardless of treatment type and outcome criteria, group was shown to be an effective treatment.
Piper & McCallum (1991)	Self-help, consciousness, cognitive restructuring, behavioral skills, dynamic	5	X	X		Grief	Group treatment has not been adequately tested to determine its efficacy.
Vandervoort & Fuhriman (1991)	Cognitive-behavioral, psychodynamic, cognitive	12	X	X		Outpatient, depression	Group efficacious in treating depressions with little evidence for differences between individual and group.

WLC = wait list control or comparable control group; OT = other group treatment comparison including pharmacotherapy; I = individual therapy comparison groups; COM = combined treatment group, e.g. group plus individual or group plus ward treatment.

(e.g., two wards in the same hospital) and hence regarded as nonequivalent (Cook & Campbell, 1979). An important common factor to note across most of the studies reviewed in the 1960s is the high proportion of institutionalized subjects. Research subjects included a high number of inpatients as well as incarcerated adults and adolescents. Anderson's (1968) review stands out as the exception in reviewing counseling groups composed primarily of students.

The first three reviews in the 1960s provided only tentative support for the efficacy of group treatment. For instance, Rickard (1962) echoed a conclusion uttered 15 years earlier (Burchard *et al.,* 1948): the tremendous variability in patients, therapists, and measures leads to an inadequate empirical test of the efficacy of group treatments. Pattison (1965) concluded that there was some behavioral support (e.g., soiling, hospital incidents, ward behavior scales) for group treatment success with institutionalized patients, but cautioned that these criteria could only loosely be related to the effect of group therapy. He reports disappointing results when psychological tests were used as dependent measures and calls for measures that match the changes targeted in group treatment. Stotsky and Zolik (1965) recommended group therapy as a helpful adjunctive treatment when combined with individual or pharmacological therapy but gave minimal support for its having an independent effect. An optimistic summary of these and contemporary conclusions (e.g., Krieger & Kogan, 1964) is that group therapy provides a strong complementary role to other more robust therapies, but it is not a robust independent treatment and should be examined by future controlled research to determine its effect.

Two later reviews (Mann, 1966; Anderson, 1968) during this decade espouse conclusions that are far more positive than the first three. The most complete review comes from Mann (1966), who critiqued more than 40 diversely conceived and executed studies and concluded that:

> regardless of the group psychotherapeutic method being tested or the instruments used to test it, the results were uniform. Change was found in approximately 45% of the studies. Thus, the present review clearly substantiates the fact that group psychotherapy does, indeed, produce objectively measurable changes in attitude, personality, and behavior. But this review does not indicate the clear superiority of one method of group psychotherapy over another; nor does it support the notion that group psychotherapy in general tends to produce only certain types of change in the patients who participate in it. (pp. 145–146)

Exactly 50% (11) of the studies used by Rickard (1962) in his inconclusive review were included in Mann's paper, yet the two authors arrived at divergent conclusions. A charitable explanation resides in Mann's mettle in simply counting the number of positive findings and essentially ignoring the fact that they came from different comparison groups, measures, and patient populations. In short, he embraced a 45% improvement rate as a respectable criterion for successful improvement.

OUTCOME STUDIES IN THE 1970S

The major reviews that followed in the next decade were based on studies that met more rigorous experimental criteria. Many of these reviewers proffered substantially different conclusions than did their predecessors (Table I). Across these seven reviews, group therapy not only consistently demonstrated its effectiveness when compared to control groups (Bednar & Kaul, 1978; Emrick, 1975; Lieberman, 1976; Luborsky, Singer, & Luborsky, 1975), but also produced comparable results to individual and alternative psychological treatments (Bednar & Kaul, 1978; Emrick, 1975; Lieberman, 1976; Luborsky et al., 1975; Meltzoff & Kornreich, 1970). These more encouraging conclusions, in contrast to those from the 1960s, may be the result of the increased rigor in investigations, movement from inpatient to diverse outpatient settings, and the emerging conceptual maturity of the field (e.g., Yalom, 1975, 1985).

Nevertheless, circumspection is warranted before one wholeheartedly adopts these conclusions. Some reviewers (Grunebaum, 1975; Parloff & Dies, 1977) during this decade still suggested that other treatment formats might be more efficacious with certain disorders. For instance, Grunebaum recommended individual treatment for phobias while Parloff and Dies deemed the treatment literature on psychoneuroses to be too embryonic to arrive at any firm conclusion. Other reviewers (Bednar & Lawlis, 1971) considered group therapy as less effective in treating patients with thought disorders, although this conclusion was challenged by later writers (e.g., Grunebaum, 1975; Kanas, 1986). An additional reason for circumspection is the lack of specificity regarding curative forces operative in group treatment that would causally account for patient improvement (Bednar & Kaul, 1978; Parloff & Dies, 1977).

OUTCOME FINDINGS FROM THE 1980S

A favorable development in the reviews of the 1980s was an increased specificity of focus. In contrast to many of the global reviews of earlier decades, in which group therapy was dealt with as an inclusive generic treatment modality, more recent reviews concentrate on either specific treatment models or populations related to specific disorders. For the most part, group therapy as a treatment format has many variations and forms. This trend is manifested in the reviews that focus on group therapy's effectiveness in treating depression, eating disorders, bereavement, schizophrenics, and the elderly, rather than heterogeneous in- or outpatient populations found in earlier review periods. Another important refinement in this decade is the nearly uniform inclusion of multiple comparison groups, including both inert and active treatment conditions; this enables reviewers to make statements regarding both general and differential efficacy of the group format.

The conclusions of the past 12 years are parallel to those of the 1970s. Group therapy demonstrated significant improvement over inert comparison groups (Freeman & Munro, 1988; Kanas, 1986; Kaul & Bednar, 1986; Vandervoort & Fuhriman, 1991; Zimpfer, 1990) and proved comparable or superior to other active treatment conditions (Cox & Merkel, 1989; Oesterheld, McKenna, & Gould, 1987; Solomon, 1983; Toseland & Siporin, 1986; Zimpfer, 1987). In a few cases, conclusions regarding the effectiveness of the group format varied from these positive conclusions. For instance, group effectiveness in dealing with clients recovering from grief could not be determined, given the limited and flawed investigations (Piper & McCallum, 1991), and a higher rate of premature termination was found for clients in group over individual format (Bostwick, 1987). Nevertheless, the general conclusion to be drawn from some 700 studies that span the past two decades is that the group format consistently produced positive effects with diverse disorders and treatment models.

SPECIAL ISSUES AND CONCERNS

This literature provides a respectable foundation upon which to build confidence in the overall effectiveness of the group treatment format. However, two concerns sully the sanguine viewpoint regarding the potency of the group format. The first concern stems from recent meta-analyses in which group therapy was shown to be inferior to other active treatments and to produce effects that were only comparable to inactive treatment conditions. The second concern lies in the frequent practice of combining group therapy with other treatments, subsequently clouding the picture in determining the independent effect of group treatment.

META-ANALYSIS

In the late 1970s, Smith and Glass (1977) applied a new review strategy to psychotherapy outcome research: meta-analysis. Briefly, meta-analysis quantifies the effectiveness of a particular form of treatment by using a common measuring standard called an *effect size*. The effect size is an estimate derived from a large number of studies that quantifies the average amount of change one could expect with a particular treatment. A primary advantage of meta-analysis is this single index of "likely" client change. This is in contrast to reporting X number of studies that demonstrate a positive or negative effect, that is, the box score method.

The past decade has produced two meta-analyses with contradictory conclusions. That is, treatment offered in a group was shown to be inferior when compared to individual therapy. Seven meta-analyses published during the past 10 years all compare the relative effectiveness of group versus individual format; some compare the group format with inert treatment conditions (Table II). Careful inspection of these meta-analyses reveals that four of the seven state conclusions that parallel the aforementioned reviews from this decade—no reliable differences were found between individual and group treatment (Miller & Berman, 1983; Robinson, Berman, & Neimeyer, 1990; Smith, Glass, & Miller, 1980; Tillitski, 1990). One of the remaining three meta-analyses (Shapiro & Shapiro, 1982) reports a slight but nonsignificant difference between the two modalities. However, the last two (Dush, Hirt, & Schroeder, 1983; Nietzel, Russel, Hemmings, & Gretter, 1987) not only report significant superiority for individual over group treatment, but also equivalent improvement profiles for patients treated in placebo control and group therapy conditions.

A comparative analysis of the individual studies that comprise these two disparate meta-analyses (Dush et al., 1983; Nietzel et al., 1987) leads to the following explanation. In contrast to the majority of the meta-analyses in Table I, the Dush and Nietzel meta-analyses rely exclusively on cognitive behavioral investigations. Moreover, careful inspection of several of the individual studies used in these two meta-analyses suggest that the majority of investigations used group as a *convenient* format to deliver predetermined treatment interventions (e.g., self-statement modification). That is, in those studies in which group treatment fared poorly, it appears that no attempt was made to incorporate or capitalize on unique properties deemed therapeutic to the group format (cf. Yalom, 1975; Bloch & Crouch, 1985). The typical investigation made no mention of attempts to facilitate traditional therapeutic factors (e.g., cohesion, universality) or to use the group-as-a-whole. Instead, the group format seems to be a convenient, cost-effective vehicle for the delivery of a treatment package originally designed for use in individual therapy. This does not necessarily suggest that such treatment orientations cannot actively utilize unique therapeutic or interpersonal factors associated with group treatment, nor does it suggest that such factors cannot naturally emerge in more structured treatments. What these studies suggest is that the treatments used in these investigations did not appear to attend to or facilitate group properties; rather they can best be described as individual treatment in the presence of others.

In contrast to the group investigations found in the Dush and Nietzel meta-analyses, most of the investigations that support the comparable efficacy of group therapy appear to highlight one or more of the unique properties of the group format. That is, rather than considering group as *a convenient and economical* format, these investigations selected group as *the* format to treat a distinct clientele or deliver a particular model of therapy based upon clinical or

TABLE II Group vs Individual Meta Analyses

Author	Treatment orientation	Group characteristics	Sample	Conclusions
Smith et. al. (1980)	Heterogeneous	Variable	Heterogeneous	The mode in which therapy was delivered made no difference in its effectiveness. Indeed, the average effects for group and individual therapy are remarkably similar. The average effect size was 0.87 for individual therapy and 0.83 for group therapy. Of the studies reviewed, 43% were individual and 49% were group.
Shapiro & Shapiro (1982)	Heterogeneous	Average time spent in therapy was 7 hours	Heterogeneous	This refined meta-analysis of the one conducted by Smith and Glass (1977) reported that, although individual therapy appeared the most effective mode ($M = 1.12$), it was closely followed by the predominant group mode ($M = 0.89$), and the only striking Tx mode finding was for couple/family therapy ($M = 0.21$).
Miller & Berman (1983)	Cognitive behavioral	Duration of treatment relatively short	Adolescents and adults, student/community volunteers & outpatients, anxious and/or depressed	This meta-analysis of 48 studies reported that cognitive behavior was equally effective in group and individual formats when compared to a nontreatment group (indiv. 0.93/group = 0.79), and when compared with other treatment controls (indiv. = 0.31/group = 0.18); it should be noted that none of the studies in the review directly compared individual with group treatment within a single study.
Dush et al. (1983)	Cognitive behavioral self-statement modification	Mean weeks of treatment were 5.9 with a range of 1–26	Approximately $1/4$ of studies used outpatients, $1/4$ used community volunteers, & $1/2$ used undergraduate depressed and anxious volunteers	Treatment modality was highly influential, with the mean effect for individual therapy nearly double that of group therapy, across all comparisons. When compared to no-treatment controls, the effect size was 0.93 for individual and 0.58 for group, and when compared to placebo controls was 0.71 for individual and 0.36 for group.

92

Study	Type of treatment	Population	Treatment length/size	Results
Nietzel et al. (1987)	Cognitive behavioral, & other	Individuals with unipolar depression, adults	Mean number of hours in treatment was 16.3, with a range of 3–69 (distribution between group and individual hours not made)	Reports a reliable difference between individual and group treatment, with group treatment being less effective. Clients treated with group ($M = 12.47$) reported more depressive symptoms than clients receiving individual treatment ($M = 10.06$).
Robinson et al. (1990)	Included treatments with verbal component (i.e., cognitive, cognitive–behavioral, & general verbal therapy)	Depressed individuals	Number of clients per group ranged from 3 to 12 ($M = 7$)	Analysis indicated that both group and individual therapy produced more improvement than no treatment, and that the effects of the two approaches were comparable. The 16 studies which compared individual/group therapy with a waitlist control, and the 15 studies which compared group with a wait list control produced nearly equal effect sizes (0.83 and 0.84, respectively).
Tillitski (1990)	Therapy, counseling, psychoeducational	Adults, adolescents, children diagnostically heterogeneous	Heterogeneous	In this reexamination of a subset of the studies looked at by Toseland and Siporin (1986), Tillitski reports finding the same average effect size for both group and individual treatment (1.35), and states that this effect was consistently greater than that of controls (0.18). Also, counseling was found to be almost twice as effective as either therapy or psychoeducation, recent studies produced larger effect sizes, and group tended to be better for adolescent and individual tended to be better for children.

conceptual grounds. Thus, when group is used as *the* format to capitalize on unique therapeutic factors operative in a group environment, it is associated with larger effects than when it is considered as a format to deliver a *singular, specific* type of treatment (e.g., cognitive–behavioral).

GROUP THERAPY COMBINED WITH OTHER TREATMENTS

The question of differential efficacy when group therapy is combined with other treatment models (e.g., individual, milieu, and drug therapy) has existed for decades. Many early writers considered group therapy appropriate only when it was combined with some other form of treatment. For instance, in an early primer for group therapy, Lewis (1947) declared that "experts in group therapy do not claim that it is a substitute for individual treatment, but feel that it is indicated in special, carefully chosen cases" (p. 10).

While many of these early writers expressed convictions based on clinical practice, a few empirical investigations were published that provided parallel support. Baehr (1954), in a study of 66 WWII hospitalized veterans, found that patients who received both individual and group therapy achieved greater gains on a self-report scale of discontentment than those patients who were treated solely with either individual or group therapy. It is important to note that these overall gains were stable when the absolute amount of time a patient spent in treatment was controlled. In a similar contemporary investigation, Powdermaker and Frank (1953) addressed the larger effect for combined therapy by trying to tease apart the independent effects of individual and group therapy. Patients treated in combined individual and group therapy were thought to derive their primary benefit first from individual therapy (57% of patients), then from group (27%), and finally, equally from both modalities (13%). It is important to note that there was no direct comparison of the two modalities in this study and that the breakdown was based on a subjective estimate of psychiatrists who were more familiar with individual treatment and hence might have been biased against the overall efficacy of group therapy.

A number of the reviews in Table I extend these early findings regarding the comparative efficacy of uniting the two formats. A robust finding from the last three decades of research is that combined individual and group treatment results in superior outcomes when compared to the independent effects of either modality (Bostwick, 1987; Freeman & Munro, 1988; Pattison, Brissenden, & Wohl, 1967). A few reviewers (Stotsky & Zolik, 1965; Anderson, 1968) have arrived at less positive conclusions, but overall, the empirical research has regarded the combined format as an effectual strategy for a wide variety of patients.

In recent years, the literature trail has moved beyond papers that attempt to determine the comparative efficacy of combining group therapy with other treatments. Rather, specific attention has focused on developing the clinical and pragmatic issues of how best to combine group with other treatments (e.g., Clarkin, Marziali, & Munroe-Blum, 1991; Lipsius, 1991; Rutan & Alonso, 1982). A harbinger of this shift was a text written by Ormont and Strean (1978) that provided a clinical treatise on how to combine individual and group therapy within a psychoanalytic framework. Porter (1980) further documents this shift by citing a dozen papers published over 14 years that chronicle both case study and conceptual support for the growing acceptance of the combined treatment format. He clarifies the difference between *combined* therapy in which the client is in both formats with the same therapist and *conjoint* therapy, in which there is simultaneous treatment in both formats by different therapists.

Several additional conceptual advancements have appeared during the last decade. An excellent example is Slavinsky-Holy's (1983) application of an object relations perspective to the combined treatment of borderline patients. She argues that the use of both modalities facilitates individuation and splitting-off from the therapist and that group therapy specifically enables the therapist to make context-relevant boundary issue interpretations. Gans (1990) provides a complementary contribution by tabulating the complex interplay of unconscious factors that occurs within patients in combined individual and group treatment. Amaranto and Bender (1990), in a fascinating reversal, explore how individual therapy can be used as a helpful adjunctive format to group therapy. With group as the primary treatment, infrequent individual therapy sessions are used to focus on members' ongoing group work and resistances that are inhibiting a productive use of the group. If significant resistances develop, more frequent individual sessions are available to assist members in the efficient use of group therapy.

A great deal of heuristically valuable conceptual material has developed over the last decade in this area. With some confidence, one can conclude that a combined approach can often be more efficacious than an independent application of one format or another. However, little understanding exists regarding the complex interplay between psychotherapeutic processes generated by combining treatments. Nevertheless, preliminary comparative process findings portend fascinating results. For instance, Brykczynska (1990), by means of a creative design, uncovered variations in the therapeutic relationship offered by the same therapist as a function of modality. Specifically, patients treated by the same therapist in either individual or group therapy systematically reported a different therapeutic relationship. More importantly, evidence from symptom reduction measures of outcome suggested that these relationship differences account for client improvement in very different ways, depending upon the modality with which the patient is being treated. Although only suggestive, these findings support some of the conceptualization just reviewed and await further empirical exploration.

REFERENCES

Amaranto, E., & Bender, S. (1990). Individual psychotherapy as an adjunct to group psychotherapy. *International Journal of Group Psychotherapy, 40* (1), 91–101.

Anderson, A. (1968). Group counseling. *Review of Educational Research, 33,* 209–226.

Baehr, G. (1954). The comparative effectiveness of individual psychotherapy, group psychotherapy, and a combination of these methods. *Journal of Consulting Psychology, 13,* 179–183.

Bednar, R., Burlingame, G., & Masters, K. (1988). Systems of family treatment: Substance or semantics? In R. Rosenweig & L. Porters (Eds.), *Annual Review of Psychology, 39* (pp. 401–434). Palo Alto, CA: Annual Reviews.

Bednar, R., & Kaul, T. (1978). Experiential group research: Current perspectives. In S. Garfield & A. Bergin (Eds.), *Handbook of psychotherapy and behavior change* (2nd ed.). New York: Wiley.

Bednar, R., & Lawlis, G. (1971). Empirical research in group psychotherapy. In A. Bergin & S. Garfield (Eds.), *The handbook of psychotherapy and behavior change.* New York: Wiley

Bloch, S., & Crouch, E. (1985). *Therapeutic factors in group psychotherapy.* Oxford: Oxford Univ. Press.

Bostwick, G. (1987). Where's Mary? A review of the group treatment dropout literature. *Social Work with Groups, 10* (3), 117–132.

Brykczynska, C. (1990). Changes in the patient's perception of his therapist in the process of group and individual psychotherapy. *Psychotherapy and Psychosomatics, 53* (1), 179–184.

Burchard, E., Michaels, J., & Kotkov, B. (1948). Criteria for the evaluation of group therapy. *Psychosomatic Medicine, 10* (3), 257–274.

Clarkin, J., Marziali, E., & Munroe-Blum, H. (1991). Group and family treatments for borderline personality disorder. *Hospital and Community Psychiatry, 42* (10), 1038–1043.

Cook, T., & Campbell, D. (1979). *Quasi-experimentation: Design and analysis issues for field settings.* Boston, MA: Houghton Mifflin.

Cox, G., & Merkel, W. (1989) A qualitative review of psychosocial treatments for bulimia. *The Journal of Nervous & Mental Disease, 177*(2), 77–84.

Dush, D., Hirt, M., & Schroeder, H. (1983). Self-statement modification with adults: A meta-analysis. *Journal of Consulting and Clinical Psychology, 94,* 408–422.

Emrick, C. (1975). A review of psychologically oriented treatment of alcoholism. *Journal for the Study of Alcoholism, 36* (1), 88–108.

Freeman, C., & Munro, J. (1988). Drug and group treatments for bulimia/bulimia nervosa. *Journal of Psychosomatic Research, 32* (6), 647–660.

Gans, J. (1990). Broaching and exploring the question of combined group and individual therapy. *International Journal of Group Psychotherapy, 40* (2), 123–137.

Grunebaum, H. (1975). A soft-hearted review of hard-nosed research on group. *International Journal of Group Psychotherapy, 25* (2), 185–197.

Kanas, N. (1986). Group psychotherapy with schizophrenics: A review of controlled studies. *International Journal of Group Psychotherapy, 36,* 339–351.

Kaul, T., & Bednar, R. (1986). Experiential group research: Results, questions & suggestions. In S. Garfield & A. Bergin (Eds.), *Handbook of psychotherapy and behavior change.* New York: Wiley.

Krieger, M., & Kogan, W. (1964). A study of group processes in the small therapeutic group. *International Journal of Group Psychotherapy, 14,* 178–188.

Lewis, N. (1947). Foreword in S. Slavson (Ed.), *The practice of group therapy.* New York: International Universities Press.

Lieberman, M. (1976). Change induction in small groups. *Annual Review of Psychology, 27,* 217–250.

Lipsius, S. (1991). Combined individual and group psychotherapy: Guidelines at the interface. *International Journal of Group Psychotherapy, 4* (3), 313–327.

Luborsky, L., Singer, B., & Luborsky, L (1975). Comparative studies of psychotherapy. *Archives of General Psychotherapy, 4(3),* 313–327.

Mann, J. (1966). Evaluation of group psychotherapy. In J. Moreno (Ed.), *The international handbook of group psychotherapy.* New York: Philosophical Library.

Meltzoff, J., & Kornreich, M. (1970). *Research in psychotherapy.* New York: Atherton Press.

Miller, R., & Berman, J. (1983). The efficacy of cognitive behavior therapies: A quantitative review of research evidence. *Psychological Bulletin, 94,* 39–53.

Nietzel, M., Russel, R., Hemmings, K., & Gretter, M. (1987). Clinical significance of psychotherapy for unipolar depression: A meta-analytic approach to social comparison. *Journal of Consulting and Clinical Psychology, 55* (2), 156–161.

Oesterheld, A., McKenna, M., & Gould, N. (1987). Group psychotherapy of bulimia: A critical review. *International Journal of Group Psychotherapy, 37* (2), 163–184.

Ormont, L., & Strean, H. (1978). *The practice of conjoint therapy: Combining individual and group treatment.* New York: Human Science Press.

Parloff, M., & Dies, R. (1977). Group psychotherapy outcome research. *International Journal of Group Psychotherapy, 27,* 281–319.

Pattison, E. (1965). Evaluation studies of group psychotherapy. *International Journal of Group Psychotherapy, 15,* (3), 382–397.

Pattison, E., Brissenden, A., & Wohl, T. (1967). Assessing specific effects of in-patient group psychotherapy. *International Journal of Group Psychotherapy, 17,* 283–297.

Piper, W., & McCallum, M. (1991). Group interventions for persons who have experienced loss: Description and evaluative research. *Group Analysis, 24,* 363–373.

Porter, K. (1980). Combined individual and group psychotherapy: A review of the literature. *International Journal of Group Psychotherapy, 30* (1), 107–114.

Powdermaker, F., & Frank, J. (1953). *Group psychotherapy: Studies in methodology of research and therapy.* Cambridge, MA: Harvard Univ. Press.

Rickard, H. (1962). Selected group psychotherapy evaluation studies. *Journal of General Psychology, 67,* 35–50.

Robinson, L., Berman, J., & Neimeyer, R. (1990). Psychotherapy for the treatment of depression: A comprehensive review of controlled outcome research. *Psychological Bulletin, 108* (1), 30–49.

Rutan, J., & Alonso, A. (1982). Group therapy, individual therapy, or both? *International Journal of Group Psychotherapy, 32* (3), 267–282.

Shapiro, D., & Shapiro, D. (1982). Meta-analysis of comparative therapy outcome studies: A replication and refinement. *Psychological Bulletin, 92,* 581–604.

Slavinsky-Holy, N. (1983). Combining individual and homogenous group psychotherapies for borderline conditions. *International Journal of Group Psychotherapy, 33* (3), 297–312.

Smith, M., & Glass, G. (1977). Meta-analysis of psychotherapy outcome studies. *American Psychologist, 32,* 752–760.

Smith, M., Glass, G., & Miller, T. (1980). *The benefits of psychotherapy.* Baltimore, MD: Johns Hopkins Univ. Press.

Solomon, S. (1983). Individual versus group therapy: Current status in the treatment of alcoholism. *Advances in Alcohol and Substance Abuse, 2* (1), 69–86.

Stotsky, B., & Zolik, E. (1965). Group psychotherapy with psychotics. *International Journal of Group Psychotherapy, 15* (3), 321–344.

Thomas, G. (1943). Group psychotherapy: A review of recent literature. *Psychosomatic Medicine, 5,* 166–180.

Tillitski, L. (1990). A meta-analysis of estimated effect sizes for group versus individual versus control treatments. *International Journal of Group Psychotherapy, 40* (2), 215–224.

Toseland, R., & Siporin, M. (1986). When to recommend group treatment. *International Journal of Group Psychotherapy, 36,* 172–201.

Vandervoort, D., & Fuhriman, A. (1991). The efficacy of group therapy for depression. *Small Group Research, 22* (3), 320–338.

Yalom, I. D. (1975/1985). *The theory and practice of group psychotherapy* (2nd/3rd eds.). New York: Basic Books.

Zimpfer, D. (1987). Groups for the aging: Do they work? *Journal for Specialists in Group Work, 12* (2), 85–92.

Zimpfer, D. (1990). Group work for bulimia: A review of outcomes. *Journal for Specialists in Group Work, 15* (4), 239–251.

CHAPTER 13

Group Therapy: a Cognitive-Behavioral Approach

SHELDON D. ROSE

In the first session of a group of young women suffering from bulimia and excessive stress, the patients are divided into pairs and asked to interview each other about their personal backgrounds and the extent and manifestation of their problem. The therapist first models the interview with one of the patients or a coleader. Then each person introduces her partner to the group. The therapist summarizes the similarities among them as well as notable differences. Later, after being provided with an overview of what they can expect to do and think about in the group, the patients are asked to read a brief case of a patient similar to themselves and then asked to write down how they are similar to and different from the example. They then report to the group what they determined. Based on this discussion, the members discuss what each would like to achieve in the course of the 12 sessions. Finally, in the first session following a model by the therapist, the patients work in pairs to design a stressful situation in which they are dissatisfied with the way they behaved. Once again, each person presents her partner's situation to the group. The session is then evaluated by the patients and the therapist. As homework, the clients are asked to develop further details in these stressful situations in terms of their thinking and their emotions which will become the focus of the next week's session.

A cognitive–behavioral group therapy (CBGT) refers to a group approach that makes use of behavioral (e.g., modeling and reinforcement), cognitive (e.g., cognitive restructuring and problem-solving), relational, and group procedures to enhance the coping skills of the participants and ameliorate relational and intrapersonal problems that patients may be experiencing. Coping skills refer to that set of behaviors and cognitions which facilitate adaptation to stressful or problematic day-to-day situations or private internal events.

Reports of the use of behavioral and cognitive therapy in groups have been mentioned as early as 1960, but for the most part, the group factor in both articles and textbooks has been ignored. There have developed a number of different models of CBGT that have evolved separately and rely on different packages of interventions for different behavioral problems. The purpose of this chapter is to describe a cognitive behavioral method in groups which also makes use of the group process.

In this chapter, we will first refer briefly to research which compares various models of CBGT to individual cognitive behavior therapy (CBT) and control group, as well as a comparison of CBGT to other types of group therapy. In comparing CBGT to individual CBT, several studies have recently appeared which support the equivalent effectiveness of individual CBT and CBGT and, usually, their somewhat greater effectiveness than control groups or alternative methods in the treatment of a variety of presenting problems. For examples of recent research which compared CGBT with individualized cognitive behavior therapy and a control group, the reader is referred to the following studies: Lee and Rush (1986) and Wolf and Crowther (1992), who treated bulimic women; Teri and Lewinsohn (1986); Scott and Stradling (1990) and Areán & Miranda (1996), who treated depression; Neron, LaCroix, and Chaput (1995), who treated patients diagnosed with panic disorder with or without agoraphobia; Fals-Stewart, Marks, and Schafer (1993), who treated patients with obsessive–compulsive disorder; Graham, Annis, Brett, and Venesoen (1996), who treated alcohol abusers; Craissati and McClurg (1997), who treated convicted perpetrators of child sexual abuse; Spence (1991), who treated patients suffering from chronic occupational pain; Onyett and Turpin (1988), who treated patients making excessive use of benzodiazine and for their anxiety; and Vollmer and Blanchard (1998), who treated patients with irritable bowel syndrome.

Support for the effectiveness of CBGT has been demonstrated in control group studies in which CBGT was compared to wait-listed and/or other approaches. Bottomly, Hunton, Roberts, and Jones (1990) demonstrated significantly improved coping styles in comparison to the other two conditions. Ehlers, Stangier, and Gieler (1995) noted significant improvements in dermatological conditions treated in cognitive–behavioral groups when compared to groups in other types of treatment. Lutgendorf, Antoni, Ironson, and Klimas (1997) report that, at the end of the 10 weeks, patients in the CBGT condition significantly decreased self-rated dysphoria, anxiety, and total distress, and the intervention also decreased *Herpes simplex* virus-typed 2 (Hsv-2) immunoglobulin G antibody titers. No such changes were found in the control group.

Subramanian (1991) found that 39 chronic pain patients in eight weekly sessions of CBGT improved significantly more than did a waiting list control (n=20) in the areas of physical and psychosocial dysfunction, though they showed no difference in the experiencing of pain.

In summary, modest support for CBGT can be identified. Usually in the control group and data-based case studies, the group factor and the cognitive–behavioral techniques are confounded, thus making interpretation of the findings unclear as to whether group or the cognitive–behavioral strategies are the major causes of change.

THE IMPLICATION OF THE GROUP IN CBGT

Originally the group was used as the context for therapy because of its convenience and efficiency in treating more than one or two people at the same time. As many scholars of group therapy have noted, it has a number of other advantages as well (e.g., Yalom, 1985, p.3). The group therapist has the opportunity to observe live interactions as opposed to solely secondhand accounts of interactions. The group provides the patient with a source of feedback about those behaviors which are irritating or acceptable to others and about those cognitions which can be viewed as distorted or dysfunctional. Yalom (1985, p. 14) also points out the importance of helping others (altruism) in facilitating therapy in groups. The patient has the opportunity to be both client and cotherapist. Although Yalom refers to insight-oriented group therapy, the same appears to be true for CBGT, provided that the therapists create conditions that permit patients to help each other. Yalom (1985, p.8) also observes that the patients discover in groups that each is not the only person with the given problem, serious as it may be. In CBGT in particular, the group provides a rich source of ideas in brainstorming, suggestions for alternative strategies, and models for role-playing. Another advantage of using the group in CBGT is the frequent and varied opportunity for mutual reinforcement which, for patients, is often far more powerful than reinforcement by a therapist.

Of course, groups are not without disadvantages. The time allotted to each individual is drastically reduced in most groups as compared to individual treatment. Thus individualization of patients may suffer. In addition, it is difficult to assure patients of the confidentiality of their comments, even though the therapist emphatically points out its importance. For this reason, some individuals in group therapy are less likely to self-disclose relevant material than they would be in individual therapy. Another danger in CBGT in particular is its tendency to become excessively didactic because of the amount of material to be disseminated. This didactic quality may reduce the cohesion of the group and also the benefits which might otherwise ensue. For this reason, in CBGT therapists in the model described here are encouraged to create as early as possible conditions that maximize patient participation and self-determination through the use of subgroup exercises.

THERAPIST ACTIVITIES IN CBGT

In CBGT, one can identify a number of sets of activities, each of which is linked to unique and overlapping therapist functions. Differentiating these sets is useful insofar as each set of activities provides a guide for the group therapist as to when emphasis should be shifted. These include a pregroup planning, orientation, assessment, intervention, generalization and termination, and followup sets of activities.

Pregroup Planning

In planning for therapy, the CBGT therapist must establish the group's purposes, assess potential membership, recruit members, decide on the group social environment or structure, and create the group's physical environment. In determining the group's purposes, the therapist can draw on several sources. Decisions must be made as to theme of the group, group size, number of therapists, frequency and length of session, the availability of a sufficient number of candidates for the group, and group composition.

In citing the literature above, it appears that most cognitive–behavioral groups have a theme, that is, all patients in the group have similar problems. Many of the homogeneous groups, though having members who are similar in presenting problems, are diverse in terms of race, gender, and ethnic background, although in most of the reports from the literature, the groups are predominantly white middle-class. Some groups are also homogeneous in terms of gender and race. Some single case (group) research and descriptions of clinical experience point to the efficacy of CBGT with Hispanics (see, e.g., Comas-Diaz & Duncan, 1985), Native-Americans (La Fromboise and Rowe, 1983; Schinke and Singer, 1994), and economically disadvantaged depressed women (Azocar, Miranda, and Dwyer, 1991). Wolfe (1987) makes use of all women's groups because consciousness raising is a component of the CBGT model she employs. Wolfe (1987) asserts that CBGT and, in particular, rational emotive therapy in groups, seems to come the closest to meeting the criteria for feminist therapy.

At least two kinds of basic organization for therapy groups can be identified. The first is open-ended groups, in which new group participants come at any time in the history of the group and leave at any time. These are usually found in institutions, although some community groups are organized in this way as well. It is a more common model with support groups than with CBGT groups. Session length varies from one to two hours.

The second type of organization is closed groups, which have a fixed beginning and fixed ending date for all participants. Most of the available research is on this type of group, and most cognitive behavioral community groups are closed. Although there are many exceptions, most closed groups last from 6 to 16 sessions once a week for one and half to two hours. The modal number is 8. In my experience, 12 to 16 sessions are required to achieve complex or multiple goals. There is usually only one group therapist, except in training situations. In the groups of adults, the modal number is 8, which permits participation by everyone at any given session and provides a wide variety of ideas and experiences. Most CBGT groups are sponsored by schools and colleges, social agencies, clinics providing mental health services, health clinics, social welfare agencies, and private practitioners.

Orientation to Group Therapy

As part of recruitment and later during the first group sessions, members are oriented to the purposes of the group, the methods to be used, the potential goals that can be achieved, and the importance of keeping what goes on in the group confidential. An overview of the group activities and expectations is presented and discussed. As part of orientation, group contracts are often developed; these contracts establish what the patients can expect from the group therapist and the agency and what the members can be expected to do. Patients are also oriented to the basic assumptions underlying each of the treatment techniques used. In this way, not only do patients know what is happening to them, expectations of positive outcomes can be stimulated.

Even during orientation, cohesion is fostered. Some means of building group cohesion are using introductory exercises in which members interview each other, keeping the tone and interaction of the group positive, providing and encouraging others to provide frequent mutual reinforcement, noting similarities as well as differences among members in terms of background and presenting concerns, keeping the group small, providing occasions for the patients to help each other, permitting and encouraging physical movement during the session, using humor, using role-playing, and providing variation in program and program media.

Assessment

Assessment is a concept central to all empirical approaches. The purpose of assessment is to determine the specific targets of interventions, the specific coping skills to be learned, in such a way as to make them amenable to intervention, the situations in which these coping skills and other target behaviors should be applied, the social and material resources of each patient which might impinge on treatment, and the potential barriers to effective treatment. It has the additional purpose of determining whether the given group or another type of therapy might be the most appropriate settling for each potential patient. Finally, assessment forms the basis for establishing the specific treatment goals within the framework of the general goals established by the agency.

The goals of CBGT may be changes in the level of intensity of specific behaviors or an increase of more general adaptive coping behaviors. Among those specific target behaviors that patients have worked on in CBGT and for which supportive research exists are reducing the extent or intensity of agoraphobia, social phobia, mood swings, obsessive–compulsive behaviors, smoking, alcohol and drug abuse, binging and purging, stress reduction, anger responses, and pain responses. Positive targets involve sleeping regularly, specific ways of making and keeping friends, increasing social activities, making more effective use of the patient's social network, improving relationships, using alternatives to aggression in expression strong feelings, and coping with serious illness, such having the HIV virus.

Cognitions refer to thoughts, images, thinking patterns, self statements, expectations, or other private or covert events which may be inferred from verbal or other overt behavior. Cognitive coping skills are those cognitions which facilitate coping with internal and social phenomena. Examples are skill in analyzing one's own cognitions, in labeling appropriately one's self-defeating self statements, in observing and rehearsing new, more appropriate self statements, and in reinforcing oneself covertly. Though important skills in their own right, some cognitive coping skills also mediate the attainment of the more observable social skills and other behaviors mentioned above or other coping behaviors. Thus, the goal of increasing cognitive coping skills is important as a means of reducing the frequency of anxiety-inducing and behavior-inhibiting cognitions, of diminishing the intensity of anxiety, and of improving social behavior (Beck and Emery, 1985; Meichenbaum, 1977). One method is keeping track of one's cognitions with such procedures as Beck's (1976) three-column techniques, in which the patient records in the first column an anxiety- or anger-producing situation; in the second, his or her automatic thoughts or thinking errors; and in the third, types of errors found in these thoughts. These are then shared with other members of the group.

Recreational and leisure time skills may be regarded as behavioral coping skills. The extent of these interests is explored in assessment to determine whether they should be amplified or modified. Although some are social in nature, they may be regarded as a separate category for coping with general life stress.

Because therapy does not go on forever, patients will have to learn to make use of their social networks more adequately. A number of social network surveys have been developed which the patients fill in to ascertain the relative helpfulness and limitations of the various social units of which they are a part (see, e.g., Rose, 1998, p. 329). In the group, they share the results of the survey with other members. Numerous other noninteractive coping skills can be explored as part of assessment, skills such as the patient's ability to manage his or her time or to relax or meditate during stressful situations.

One can not learn coping skills in a vacuum. One must identify the specific situations with which the individual must learn to cope. To this end, the group members are taught to identify and define their unique problematic situations. The therapist first provides models of such situations, which the members discuss in terms of the criteria for formulating situations they have thus far had trouble dealing with. They provide feedback to each other on how well they have learned the following criteria: that it is important to the patient and likely to occur again, that it be specific as to time and place and the people involved, and that is represents a situation the patient might have difficulty in dealing with. After discussion of the application of these principles to the model situations, as an extragroup task it is suggested that each person develop one or more such situations to be presented at the following session in the group in terms of how well each situation meets the criteria. The group therapist develops a set of predetermined or "canned" situations for those members who can not develop one for themselves.

As part of assessment and to determine the progress of treatment, data on patient behavior and the resolution of problems are usually systematically collected before, throughout, immediately following therapy, and several weeks or months after therapy. In order to understand patients' responses, session by session, to the program as a whole, a postsession questionnaire is filled out by each patient and the therapist at the end of each session. In summary, some of the methods of collecting data mentioned above include diaries, personality inventories and checklists, role-play tests, sociometric tests, self observation, direct observations of the group or of individuals when not in the group, possession questionnaires, and interviews. (Each of these is discussed in more detail in Rose, 1989, pp. 109–136, for adults and Rose, 1998, 130–151, for adolescents). The more structured methods permit evaluation of outcome and process.

Based on the initial data collected in the first part of assessment, goals are eventually established together with the patient. These goals usually are in terms of the specific target behaviors and cognitions that the patients need to achieve by the end of treatment and the coping behaviors required to deal with the problem situations. Knowing each other well because of their intense interaction, the group members provide each other with ideas as to goals each might pursue and feedback as to whether the goals have been formulated in terms of the following criteria: the goal is important and achievement is realistic, a time frame is provided (e.g., by the end of treatment or by next month), and the goal is sufficiently specific that the patient knows when where it has to be achieved. If necessary, subgoals may also be formulated. Two examples of sets of related specific treatment goals meeting the above criteria are:

1. (For the depressed patient) By the end of treatment, I will participate in at least two social activities every week with friends or family members. I will also identify any self-defeating thoughts I make and will change each into a coping thought. On my self-monitoring card, I will score an average of 5 or lower on the 10-point depression scale.

2. (For the abusive male) By the end of treatment, when I begin to feel angry, I will take a deep breath and let it out slowly and remind myself that I can destroy my marriage if I give in to it. When I experience the first signs of anger with my wife, I will excuse myself from the situation and walk away. I will also increase the number of compliments I make to my wife to a minimum of once a day.

Once goals are formulated, an additional means of measurement can be used to ascertain progress toward goals, goal attainment scaling (see Cardillo, 1994). The goal attainment scales are developed in the group, with the members helping each other in subgroup exercises. Following the formulation of goals, group programs and interventions can be planned which facilitate the achievement of these goals.

Intervention

Base on the goals, intervention strategies are selected which are likely to facilitate change from or maintenance of present levels. In order to develop these and specific behavioral and coping skills, usually no one intervention technique is sufficient. A number of methods of teaching patients necessary specific skills include problem-solving, modeling, rehearsal, coaching, cognitive-restructuring, rational–emotive techniques, socio-recreational, relaxation training, and small group techniques. In CBGT, most of these methods, with special emphasis on how they are used in a group, are combined into one integrated approach, A method is selected for inclusion if it has some independent empirical foundation and a specific relationship to the above-mentioned targets. In the section on interventions, each of these will be briefly described.

Generalization

Generalization, a concern of all therapies, refers to the process of transferring what the patient has learned in the group to the outside world and maintaining what he or she has learned beyond the end of therapy. The most fundamental principle of generalization is that it rarely occurs without taking steps to see that it occurs (Stokes and Baer, 1977). One of the major strategies in

CBGT for transferring learning from the group to other situations involves the use of extragroup tasks which are designed at the end of every session to be carried out between sessions and reported back to the group.

In addition, the patients are prepared to deal with persons who might be unsympathetic to their changes. Former patients are sometimes brought in to discuss the possibilities of setbacks and how they might be handled. Possible self-referral sources are discussed, such as a counselor, local clinic, or health service. Finally, as part of this phase, a followup or "booster"session would be held two or three months following therapy.

Members are finally prepared for termination by their developing a plan as to how they intend to apply what they learned in the group when the group ends, and by designing activities appropriate to practicing their learned skills. These plans often contain such actions as joining a nontherapeutic group, reading a self-help book, practicing relaxation on a regular basis, meeting with a group member to talk about the principles learned in the group, and meeting again for a booster session.

In order to diminish the intensity of the relationship of the members to each other and to the group therapist as the group approaches termination, members are encouraged to establish relationships outside of the group and to become involved in extragroup activities, such as family activities, bowling leagues, bridge clubs, dancing lessons, and social organizations. Furthermore, relationships to nongroup members are encouraged. Extragroup tasks gradually become less structured but more demanding. Social, recreational, and other cohesion-building activities are held to a minimum as the group approaches termination.

INTERVENTION STRATEGIES USED IN CBGT

The most common intervention strategies used in CBGT are systematic problem-solving, the modeling sequence, cognitive change procedures, relaxation and meditation, and small group techniques. (Some therapists may also use other cognitive behavior procedures such as imagery, group desensitization, group exposure, and reinforcement strategies which are not defined below.)

Systematic Problem-Solving

Systematic problem-solving is a method central to CBGT insofar as patients bring problematic situations of concern to the group and the group, under the guidance of the therapist, attempts to help them find solutions to those problems. It is systematic insofar as the members follow (or deviate by plan from) specified steps. The steps characteristic of the problem-solving process include orienting the members to the basic assumptions of problem-solving, defining the problem, generating alternative solutions, selecting the best set of solutions, planning and preparing for implementation, implementing the solution, and evaluating the outcome. (These steps are adapted from the work of D'Zurilla, 1986.)

Within the framework of problem-solving, several other cognitive and behavioral procedures are used to prepare the group members to implement the solutions to which they are agreed. One of the most important is the modeling sequence.

The Modeling Sequence

This sequence is designed to teach specific interactive behaviors for coping with various problem situations, and includes such techniques as overt modeling, behavior rehearsal, coaching, and group feedback. Modeling refers to learning that occurs through the observation of a model, who might be the group therapist, another member of the group, someone in the patient's environment, or an admired person on stage, on screen, in novels, or in public life. Modeling may be role-played in the group or it may be observed directly in real life. Modeling as a procedure is derived from social learning theory, for which Bandura (1977) has found extensive empirical support. Modeling is specifically used to demonstrate how a situation problematic to one or more patients in the group may be handled effectively. Behavioral rehearsal is role-play technique in which a patient, having observed a model, practices new, more effective ways of handling a problem situation. Coaching refers to instructions, verbal, or physical cues given to the patient when she or he is modeling or rehearsing a set of behaviors in a given situation. Group feedback is the verbal evaluation from others as to how effectively the patient role-played or modeled. Following the modeling sequence, the patient prepares for and carries out extragroup tasks to practice the newly learned coping skill in the real world. All these steps are demonstrated in the example below.

> Following the analysis of the situation calling for a refusal of drink when offered, the therapist asks the group members for possible responses to the one of agreeing with the friend and going with him, which is what the patient, Pete, had done in original event. Based on the suggestions of his fellow patients, Pete decided that he would like to refuse clearly and in a matter-of-fact tone of voice, reminding his friend that he (Pete) was on the wagon and was working hard to stay there and he would appreciate whatever help his friend could give him. Pete would repeat the statement if pressured further. The therapist set the scene outside a bar, and then modeled the situation with one of the other group members acting as the friend. Then Pete, who felt that one demonstration was enough, played himself and his friend was played by the same person as in the first role-play. When it was finished, the therapist asked the other patients to tell Pete what he did well and then what he might consider doing differently. The members responded that Pete made an impressive statement and didn't argue. They suggested that he might consider giv-

ing better eye contact and speaking in a more matter-of-fact tone of voice. Pete rehearsed one more time trying to incorporate the suggestions with the "friend" in the role-play being much more insistent.

Cognitive Change Methods

Cognitive change methods refer to the steps taken to train the patient in more effective ways of thinking about or evaluating him- or herself as the patient responds in specific problematic situations. In groups, many different cognitive procedures are used, often in combination with each other and with other types of procedures such as the modeling sequence. It is assumed that in a given set of circumstances, cognitions, in part, mediate overt behavioral and affective responses. These cognitions include how one values oneself and one's action and how one specifically thinks in or evaluates a given situation. In CBGT, the most commonly used cognitive procedures are cognitive restructuring (Beck, 1976) and rational emotive therapy (Ellis and Wyden, 1997).

Cognitive Restructuring is characterized by two sets of procedures. First, one set of procedures is to identify the distorted patterns of thinking and/or dysfunctional schemata (Beck, 1976) which interfere with social functioning or create intense emotions. Second, a set of methods is used to replace this distorted or dysfunctional thing with self statements that facilitate effective coping with day-to-day life events and reduce anxiety and stress. In the first set of procedures, the patients are trained by means of group exercises to identify cognitive distortions in case examples and to label them into such categories as absolutizing, catastrophizing, mind-reading, selective perception, or prophesizing (Beck, 1976).

Once the distorted thinking is identified and labeled, each patient, assisted by the other group members, is asked to replace the distortions with coping statements. Group exercises are used to facilitate this replacement, in which the patients first correct in the list of "canned" statements is presented as points of departure. For example, "If I take one step at time, I can handle this," or "I should remind myself to take a deep breath and relax," or "If I make a mistake, it's not so terrible; nobody is perfect."

Once the members become skilled in replacing cognitive distortions with coping statements on simulated examples, they can begin, with the help of the group, to replace distorted thoughts of their own with coping statements.

Finally, the members assign each other tasks to perform outside of the group to try out and self-monitor their use of coping self statements to replace cognitive distortions. At a subsequent session, each patient reports back his or her observations to the group.

Rational–Emotive Therapy (Ellis & Dryden, 1997) is another form of cognitive restructuring that is often used in groups. The author believes that most maladaptive behavior has at its roots distorted thinking characterized by arbitrariness and inaccurate assumptions about others and self. It is often preoccupied with "musts," e.g., I must not disappoint my parents. I must be a big success." The role of the therapist is to help the client and the group members to help each other recognize these fundamental, but mistaken, beliefs, and then to help each other exchange them for constructive beliefs. In therapy, the therapist actively questions and points out contradictions and inconsistencies and, in groups, encourages the members to do it for each other.

Other methods with cognitive as well as behavioral elements used in groups are thought stopping in the face of persistent recurring thoughts, systematic desensitization or exposure methods in the case of phobias, and guided imagery. Gradual exposure methods have been used in the treatment of agoraphobia (Hand, LaMontagne, and Marks, 1974) and obsessive compulsive disorder (Fals-Stewart *et al.*, 1993) with positive results.

Relaxation Methods

These are strategies for helping patients to cope with strong emotional responses such as anger, stress, or depression. The training involves teaching patients a modified version of the alternate tension and relaxation technique (developed by Jacobsen, 1929, and adapted by Bernstein and Borkovec, 1983) and then later fading the tension phases. Variations uniquely adapted to various populations are also taught. In addition, meditation (Carrington, 1978) and diaphragmatic breathing are taught in some groups as alternatives to deep muscle relaxation. Members of the group monitor each other, so that they are both learners and teachers. They are given tapes to use at home in order to encourage greater practice.

Small Group Procedures

Because CBGT is also a small group approach, it is possible to take advantage of the many procedures which enhance the process either because they occur in the context of the group of because they are unique to the group setting. Since most group therapies make use of some of these techniques, I shall illustrate only a few in terms of their unique application in CBGT. These include cohesion building (already mentioned), role-playing, the buddy system, subgrouping, leadership delegation, and group exercises. (These and other group procedures commonly used in CBGT are described in detail by Rose, 1989, as they apply to adults and Rose, 1998, as they apply to children.)

Identifying and Resolving Group Problems

In all groups, one can observe a number of group problems. These can be defined as an intragroup interactive event (or series of events) or a product of interactive events which interferes with effective member task performance or goal attainment. The responsibility for achieving a change in group process can not usually be linked to a change in behavior of any one member or of the group therapist, but to interactive changes among all or most of the members and the therapist. Several problems, in particular, stand out, such as when the group cohesion is too low, when the communication pattern is directly primarily from members to the therapist and not to each other, when the self-disclosure is too low, when some members dominate the interaction while others are virtually excluded, when antitherapeutic norms exist such as a pattern of lateness, where members are too critical or too protective of one another, and where members are frequently off-task. In general, most of these group problems are avoided by careful treatment programming. Some problems can be dealt with by checking with members to see whether they perceive the problem or not and how they feel and think about it. Sometimes, this can be used as an opportunity to correct inappropriate expectations or other cognitive distortions using the above-mentioned cognitive restructuring techniques. Occasionally, when a group problem still persists, it is possible to use systematic problem-solving.

SUMMARY AND CONCLUSION

In this chapter, the reader has been presented with one type of cognitive–behavioral group therapy, in which use is explicitly made of the group as well as cognitive and behavioral strategies of intervention. As demonstrated by the literature, a large body of empirical research exists for CBGT for diverse problems and populations. The various assessment, intervention, and generalization strategies most commonly employed in CBGT have been presented while taking advantage of the group context. The cornerstone of using the group in CBGT is maximum involvement of the members in the treatment process through the use of small subgroup exercises (Rose, 1999a,b) in which the clients first apply the behavioral and cognitive strategies to simulated cases and eventually to aspects of their own situations. The ultimate focus on treatment is generalized cognitive, emotional, and behavioral change under predetermined conditions. These results are evaluated at termination and followup to determine the effectiveness of therapy.

REFERENCES

Areán, P., & Miranda, J. (1996). The treatment of depression in elderly primary care patients: A naturalistic study. *Journal of Clinical Geropsychology, 2,* 153–160.
Azocar, F., Miranda, J., & Dwyer, E. V. (1991). Treatment of depression in disadvantaged women. *Women and Therapy, 18* (3–4), 91–105.

Bandura, A. (1977b). *Social learning theory.* Englewood Cliffs, NJ: Prentice-Hall. Beck, A. T. (1976). *Cognitive therapy and emotional disorders.* New York: International Universities Press.

Beck, A. T., & Emery, G. (1985). *Anxiety disorders and phobias.* New York: Basic Books.

Bernstein D. A., & Borkovec, T. D. (1973). *Progressive relaxation training: A manual for the helping professions.* Champaign, IL: Research Press.

Bottomley, A., Hunton, S., Roberts, G., & Jones, L. (1996). A pilot study of cognitive behavioral therapy and social support group interventions with newly diagnosed cancer patients. *Journal of Psychosocial Oncology 14*(4), 65–83.

Cardillo, J. E. (1994). Goal setting, follow-up, and goal monitoring. In T.J., Kiresuk, A. Smith, & J. E. Cardillo, (Eds.), Goal attainment scaling: Applications, theory, and measurement (pp. 39–59). Hillsdale, NJ: L. Erlbaum Assoc.

Carrington, P. (1978). *Learning to mediate: Clinically standardized meditation (CSM). Course workbook.* Kendall Park, NJ: Pace Educational Systems.

Comas-Diaz, L., & Duncan, J. W. (1985). The cultural context: A factor in assertiveness training with mainland Puerto Rican women. *Psychology of Women Quarterly, 9,* 463–475.

Craissati, J., & McClurg, G. (1997). The challenge project: A treatment program evaluation for perpetrators of child sexual abuse. *Child Abuse & Neglect, 21,* 637–648.

D'Zurilla, T. J. (1986). *Problem-solving therapy: Social competence approach to clinical intervention.* New York: Springer Press.

Ellis, A., & Dryden, W. (1997). *The practice of rational–emotive behavior therapy* (2nd ed.). New York: Springer Publishing Company.

Ehlers, A., Stangler, U., & Gieler, U. (1995). Treatment of atopic dermatitis: A comparison of psychological and dermatological approaches to relapse prevention. *Journal of Consulting and Clinical Psychology 63*(4), 624–635.

Fals-Stewart, W., Marks, A. P., & Schafer, J. (1993). A comparison of behavioral group therapy and individual behavior therapy in treating obsessive–compulsive disorder. *The Journal of Nervous and Mental Disease, 181*(3), 189–193.

Hand, I., LaMontagne, Y., & Marks, I.M. (1974). Group exposure (flooding) *in vivo* for agoraphobics. *British Journal of Psychiatry, 124,* 588–602.

Graham, K., Annis, H., Brett, P., & Venesoen, P. (1996). A controlled field trial of group versus individual cognitive–behavioural training for relapse prevention. *Addiction, 91,* 1127–1139.

Jacobsen, E. (1929). *Progressive relaxation.* Chicago: University of Chicago Press.

LaFromboise, T., & Rowe, W. (1983). Skills training for bicultural competence: Rationale and application. *Journal of Counseling Psychology, 30,* 589–595.

Lee, N. F., & Rush, A. J. (1986). Cognitive–behavioral group therapy for bulimia. *International Journal of Eating Disorders May 5*(4), 599–615.

Lutgendorf, S. K., Antoni, M. H., Ironson, G., Klinas, N. (1997). *Journal of Consulting and Clinical Psychology 65*(1), 31–43.

Meichenbaum, D. (1977). *Cognitive–behavior modification.* New York: Plenum Press.

Neron, S., LaCroix, D., & Chaput, Y. (1995). Group vs. individual cognitive behaviour therapy in panic disorder: An open clinical trial with a six month follow-up. *Canadian Journal of Behavioural Science, 27,* 379–392.

Onyett, S. R., & Turpin, G. (1988) Benzodiazepine withdrawal in primary care: A comparison of behavioural group training and individual sessions. *Behavioural-Psychotherapy, 16* (4), 297–312.

Rose, S. D. (1999a). Group therapy with adults: A cognitive behavioral interactive approach: A training manual for therapists. Madison, WI: School of Social Work, University of Wisconsin.

Rose, S. D. (1998). *Group therapy with troubled youth.* Thousand Oaks, CA: Sage.

Rose, S. D. (1989). *Working with adults in groups: A multimethod approach.* San Francisco: Jossey-Bass.

Schinke, S. P., & Singer, B. R. (1994) Prevention of health care problems. In D. K. Grand (Ed.) *Cognitive and behavioral treatment* (pp. 285–298). Belmont, CA: Brooks/Cole.

Scott, M., & Stradling, S. (1990). Group cognitive therapy for depression produces clinically significant reliable change in community-based settings. *Behavioural Psychotherapy, 18.*

Stokes, T. F., & Baer, D. M. (1977). An implicit technology of generalization. *Journal of Applied Behavior Analysis, 10,* 349–367.

Spence, S. H. (1991). Cognitive–behaviour therapy in the treatment of chronic, occupational pain of the upper limbs: A 2 yr follow-up. *Behaviour Research and Therapy Vol 29*(5), 503–509.

Subramanian, K. (1991). Structured groupwork for the management of chronic pain: An experimental investigation. *Research on Social Work Practice, 1,* 32–45.

Teri, L., & Lewinsohn, P. M. (1986). Individual and group treatment of unipolar depression: Comparison of treatment outcome and identification of predictors of successful treatment outcome. *Behavior-Therapy Jun 17*(3), 215–228.

Vollmer, A., & Blanchard, E. (1998). Controlled comparison of individual versus group cognitive therapy for irritable bowel syndrome. *Behavior Therapy, 29,* 19–33.

Wolf, E. M., & Crowther, J. H. (1992). An evaluation of behavioral and cognitive–behavioral group interventions for the treatment of bulimia nervosa in women. *International Journal of Eating Disorders, 11* (1), 3–15.

Wolfe, J. L. (1987). Cognitive behavioral group therapy for women. In C.M. Brody (Ed.), *Women's therapy groups: Paradigms of feminist treatment* (pp. 163–173). New York: Springer.

Yalom, I. D. (1985). *The theory and practice of group psychotherapy* (3rd ed.) New York: Basic Books.

CHAPTER 14

Psychodynamic Group Psychotherapy*

J. Scott Rutan and Walter N. Stone

It was the first session of a long-term psychodynamic group; the eight members committed to an initial 15 sessions as part of the contract. The group was moving along in typical fashion for a first session, asking why people were there, revealing superficial aspects of their lives, etc., when a male member took out a large pocket knife and began to clean his nails with it. I asked him to put the knife away, and he protested, asking me why and saying that he had a right to use his knife if he wasn't harming anyone. I said, "Then you don't plan on using that for protection?" He laughed and said, "From who?"

I told him that he was going to be very useful to the group with helping people to express individuality and question authority. "But," I asked, "who do you expect will clean up your nail droppings, me, or the members, or yourself?" He then said he hadn't thought about that and put his knife away. He began to brush the droppings into his hand and carefully threw them, wrapped in a Kleenex, into the garbage pail. The group then began to process this critical incident as the session went on.

A neophyte group therapist observing two groups, one having been in existence for three or four sessions and the other for several years, would quickly be able to distinguish between their functioning. What development has occurred that accounts for this change? Understanding the predictable broad outlines of group evolution, complete with the tasks involved in the various stages of that evolution, provides an anchor for the therapist. Just as a knowledgeable individual therapist can gain a deeper understanding of his patients'

---

* Reprinted with permission from Rutan, J.S., & Stone, W.N. (1993). Group development. *Psychodynamic Group Psychotherapy.* New York: Guilford Press.

ideas and associations by having an appreciation for the developmental levels and the associated tasks for individuals as they grow, so group therapists are helped by an understanding of the usual stages of group development.

Like individuals, groups do not move forward in a linear fashion; they are subject to forward and backward movement. Furthermore, these fluctuations do not take place automatically or on any set timetable.

Group development is a product of the individual members, their interactions among themselves and with the therapist. Nonetheless, accurate assessment of the developmental level can aid the therapist in attempts to notice shifts in groupwide functioning. In some situations, patients with preoedipal conflicts or with significant developmental arrests may make major therapeutic gains while working on the early issues of joining and belonging to a group. These patients derive the most therapeutic benefit when the group members are examining aspects of building trust and belonging. For patients who have conflicts at a more advanced individual developmental level, there is less therapeutic gain at early levels of group development. If a group is composed entirely of patients with preoedipal problems, that group will likely remain at early levels of development for prolonged periods, which would be quite beneficial to such patients. On the other hand, if healthier patents remained stuck in an early stage of development for a prolonged period, this would constitute either a case of misdiagnosis or significant problems of transference of countertransference.

As discussed earlier, some therapists reify group development and focus on little else, as, for example, do the strict followers of Bion. The stages of development are indicators that help the therapist understand more fully what is going on in the group. One stage is not inherently more valuable than another. A common misconception among therapists is that, in order to have a "good" group, it is imperative that the group must attain and maintain the most advanced developmental level. For many patients, this would be asking the impossible. Rather, there should be a reasonable fit between the level of group development and the dynamic issues salient for the members.

A major portion of the knowledge about group development emerged from studies of time-limited, closed-membership groups (Tuckman, 1965). Generalization of these ideas to ongoing, open-membership psychotherapy groups has often been done indiscriminately. There is overlap, but the two situations are not identical. For instance, a psychotherapy group has only one actual beginning. Yet, with the additions of one or more new members, there are modified new beginnings repeatedly, each usually accompanied by the reemergence of themes and modes of relating similar to those at the time of the initial sessions. Similarly, events inside or outside an ongoing group may set off recrudescences of power struggles characteristic of the second phase of development. The repetition of various developmental phases provides an opportunity to rework previously traversed ground, sometimes in greater depth and with increased insight, and, therefore, has considerable therapeutic potential. Keep in mind the reality that these are schematic presentations; only the careful study of processes in each particular group, as well as the dynamics of individuals involved, will provide the base for meaningful therapeutic change.

Not everyone endorses the concept of development within groups. Slavson (1957) attempted to expunge group processes from psychotherapeutic groups; he focused instead purely on interpersonal interactive processes. Slavson's position represents an effort to transpose classical dyadic psychoanalytic concepts (transference and resistance) into the group psychotherapy setting. By linking group interaction closely to dyadic therapy, Slavson and others (Wolf & Schwartz, 1962) stressed the continuity of psychodynamic/psychoanalytic concepts. This historic bridge made group therapy acceptable, if not attractive, to the mainstream of the American psychotherapeutic community.

Gradually, the tradition of linking individual psychodynamics to group psychotherapy included the transposition of individual developmental stages to groups. Group development came to be seen as replicating oral, anal, and phallic stages. (Saravay, 1975; Gibbard & Hartman, 1973). Using such traditional analytic metaphors does not do justice to the complex phenomena observable in groups; an expanded perspective that encompasses the more complex data of individual and group interactions is necessary. Within the group matrix are a variety of relationships—among the members, between the members and the leader, and between the members and the group as a whole. These patterns develop in a rather characteristic fashion.

One of the tasks for members is to determine what will make their efforts in the group most useful. When a new group forms, these tasks are unknown, and the members, through trial and error, discover what are helpful tasks, roles, and norms. That learning becomes reflected in shifts in how the members relate and examine themselves and their relationships to each other and the leader.

Thus far, no schema describing group development has been able to do justice to the complexity of internal fantasies and behavioral transactions that occur when a small group of individuals organizes and begins to work together (Hill & Gruner, 1973). However, two elements are always present in successful groups: accomplishing the goal and, simultaneously, attending to the emotional needs of the members. In group psychotherapy, where the goal is improved emotional functioning of the members, the overlap with the group task is extensive. Nonetheless, the components can be separated, and it serves a heuristic purpose to do so.

An individual's attainment of goals and fulfillment of emotional needs are central considerations in group development and can be seen as occurring in three phases: the first phase consists of the reaction to joining and forming the group; the second phase consists of the reaction to feelings of belonging; and the third phase is the stabilization of the mature working group. In the third phase, the members have a consistent image of what is necessary to attain therapeutic goals. It is important for therapists to remember that the ultimate goals of therapy—improved intrapsychic functioning and self-learning—can occur during any of these three stages.

SUMMARY

The concept of group development is valuable in orienting therapists to a number of processes common to group psychotherapy. Familiarity with the phases of development helps anchor therapists in their work and provides a road map to help them understand what is occurring within their groups.

A great deal of valuable therapeutic work can be accomplished in each phase. Indeed, each phase offers unique opportunities. Further, since groups are dynamic organisms composed of living beings, the phases are not rigid and steadfast. The stages are best considered guidelines, not laws. As groups grow and are confronted with crisis and change, the phases will be revisited regularly.

As development takes place, each group forms its particular culture and norms which have a major impact upon how the group goes about fulfilling its goal of helping the members solve their problems. The therapist has considerable importance in the evolution of the culture, but the members also contribute greatly. The concept of role is linked with group requirements for building and maintaining its culture, as well as with the individual's past habitual methods of handling stress and anxiety. Both aspects of role require consideration and frequently can be observed as overlapping within the group.

REFERENCES

Gibbard, G. S., & Hartman, J. S. (1973). The Oedipal paradigm in group development: A clinical and empirical study. *Small Group Behavior, 4*, 305–354.

Hill, W., & Gruner, L. (1973). A study of development in open and closed groups. *Small Group Behavior, 4*, 355–381.

Saravay, S. (1975). Group psychology and the Structural Theory: A revised psychoanalytic model of group therapy. *Journal of the American Psychoanalytic Association, 23*, 69–89.

Slavson, S. R. (1957). Are there group dynamics in therapy groups? *International Journal of Group Psychotherapy, 7*, 115–130.

Tuckman, B. W. (1965). Developmental sequence in small groups. *Psychological Bulletin, 63*, 384–399.

Wolf, A., & Schwartz, E. K. (1962). *Psychoanalysis in groups.* New York: Grune and Stratton.

CHAPTER 15

Redecision Therapy*

JOHN GLADFELTER

I work one-to-one in group. And sometimes, I switch places, as the therapist, with another group member who also works one-to-one. In one session, Joe was working on his problems with authority. Michael asked him: "Wouldn't it be a good idea to talk to the 'father in your head' about your problems with authority?"

I asked Michael to lead some two-chair work with Joe. So Joe got in his chair in the center of the circle, Michael put a chair facing Joe, and Michael directed Joe in switching from one chair, Michael's, to the other chair, the father in Michael's head.

When their work terminated, with Michael feeling much relief, there was applause from the entire group. Victory was announced.

Redecision therapy is an approach to group psychotherapy developed by Robert and Mary Goulding (1979), based on their creative efforts in combining transactional analysis (TA) and Gestalt therapy with a wealth of clinical experience. Transactional analysis is the treatment method for working with groups created by Eric Berne (1961, 1966a, 1966b, 1972). There are three approaches: classical, cathexis, and redecision therapy. Gestalt therapy is a treatment technique developed by Frederick Perls (1969), based on awareness and the capacity for emotional change.

The redecision approach to treatment is more than a combination of the two modalities. It is a uniquely powerful approach to group psychotherapy that combines the cognitive clarity of TA with the affective engagement of Gestalt therapy. Many members of the American Group Psychotherapy Association

---

* Reprinted with permission from Gladfelter, J. (1992). Redecision therapy. *International Journal of Group Psychotherapy* 42(3), 319–334.

have learned redecision therapy through the active involvement of Robert and Mary Goulding in the Association's workshops and institutes.

Making a comparison of redecision therapy and other group therapies is difficult. Berne's (1966b) departure from traditional psychological and psychiatric language was a significant linguistic and conceptual change. He believed that psychological language had become too complicated. He went about finding common words for his group treatment and taught the people who worked and trained with him to speak "Martian." He believed that the language should approximate the real events and experiences common to most people. His goal was to use language that a person coming to this planet without social and cultural indoctrination would be able to understand, a language about feelings, thinking, and behavior.

Redecision therapy follows the TA tradition, and therapists pay close attention to words and what they mean. For example, "to try" is not "to do" and "can't" does not mean "won't." It is important to listen carefully to what the patient means by what he or she says.

There are many conceptual and philosophical disparities between redecision therapy and other group therapies. Therefore, a brief explanation of the theory and techniques is in order. The redecision method is based on the transaction theory of ego states, games, transactions, and scripts. The Adult ego state is that part of the personality that processes data and is often thought of as the computer. The Child ego state is that part that is young and emotional. The Parent ego state is that part of people that acts and talks like parents and can be serious or nurturing. The Child ego state is thought of as having two components: the Free Child, which is little, happy, and fun-loving, and the Adapted Child, which is looking for a way to adapt to a grownup and parental world. Games are those interchanges between people that repeatedly result in their feeling bad and blaming others. Transactions are those communicative interchanges between the ego states of two or more persons which may contain both social and psychological messages. A social message is the meaning content of the message, and the psychological message is the emotion and value content. A script is a life plan, chosen early by the Child ego state, that enables the child to survive and can result in maladaptive behavior for an adult. The early decision of the Child ego state is the beginning point of the script.*

Redecision therapy introduces several concepts to the language of transactional analysis, including impasse, injunction, contact, contract, and anchoring. An impasse is a place where an individual becomes stuck. The person finds himself or herself in a situation in which clear thought is difficult, uncomfortable, emotions are experienced, and the Child ego state prevails, making the

---

* Note use of capital letters when referring to ego states (Parent, Adult, Child). Lowercase letters indicate real-life parent, adult, child.

individual unable to change what he or she says or does. Contact is a special way of meeting and engaging the Child, Adult, and Parent ego states in the treatment process. Contact goes beyond rapport and involves the therapist's becoming a powerful and nurturing individual, to whom the patient bonds. In contact, the three ego states of the therapist make connection with the ego states of the patient. Anchoring is the embedding of a feeling in a way that enables the patient to reexperience that feeling by choice: The patient begins the process of change and experiences new positive feelings; the therapist then helps the patient anchor the feeling by using cues or touching. This behavioral technique not only allows the patient to reexperience the feeling, it helps him or her to give up negative feelings that were anchored in the past. Stewart and Joines' (1987) book, *TA Today,* provides detailed descriptions of the transactional analysis concepts and other TA approaches to group treatment.

John McNeel (1977) discusses the conceptual components of redecision therapy in his doctoral research on the approach. Briefly stated, the goals of the approach are (a) that patients reclaim power and responsibility for their lives, (b) that patients make changes in themselves in a nurturing and therapeutic environment, (c) that the therapist models important ways of living and being, (d) that the thinking errors of patients are consistently confronted, (e) that incongruities in behavior and thinking are confronted, (f) that modified Gestalt chair techniques are used to engage the patients' bad feelings, and (g) that the group operates on the basis of clear rules established by the therapist.

Therapists who use transactional analysis and redecision therapy are firmly committed to a developmental viewpoint. Throughout the range of techniques employed, therapists attend to the early decisions made from the Child ego state. From early in life, children make decisions about their feelings, their thinking, and their behavior. They experience parental influence and make their choices based on their own interpretation of the world. Recent literature on early childhood development supports this view (Stern, 1985). Change must, therefore, come from that Child ego state that made the early decisions. In the therapy group, the patient feels supported, nurtured, and capable of changing those early decisions. A variety of therapeutic techniques from other approaches, such as psychodrama, behavior therapy, and cognitive therapy, are incorporated into redecision therapy. They serve to enable the patient to use childhood experiences and alter the choices made at an early time in life.

The treatment work of the Gouldings is done primarily in a marathon setting (Goulding, 1977). The marathon group can be excellent in the amount of therapeutic energy, support, and continuity it can provide. It does not, however, lend itself to the lifestyles of most patients. The Gouldings' work has also been successfully employed in private practice by many therapists (Gladfelter, 1977). In such a setting, groups meet for 2-hour sessions on a weekly basis, as is customary in private or clinic practice. Other therapists have noted that redecision therapy is effective for working with couples' groups, homogeneous groups, and time-limited groups (Kadis, 1985). In particular, the philosophy and concepts of redecision therapy have led to a view of psychotherapy that integrates many of the skills and beliefs of newer psychotherapeutic approaches (Gladfelter, 1990).

In a redecision therapy group, the therapist works one-to-one with group members. The group benefits through contagion of affect from the patient who is working with the therapist. They also benefit through learning how to work with the therapist and how to be a patient. The group acts in a supportive and nurturing fashion and gives positive feedback to the patient who has finished working. Applause, hugging, and thoughtful positive comments are a part of the backing given to each patient.

In making contact during the patient's first visit, the therapist needs to offer change, no matter how strange or incongruent such a notion might be. This may be the only individual session that the patient has with the therapist, so the therapist must be skilled in making contact. Goulding and Goulding (1978) quote Berne in saying that the therapist's goal in treatment should be the cure of the patient in the first visit. This may seem unrealistic, yet the goal is to support an individual's Adapted Child, who may be feeling hopeless, help-less, and distressed. Part of the patient is looking for someone who can both appreciate the patient for what he or she is and help bring about change. The patient may also believe that the therapist will effect the change. At this point, the therapist must emphasize that they will be working together in a group, and also that the patient has the power, with the help of the therapist, to change. If the patient feels heard and understood by the therapist, the begin-ning group experience will be positive.

Developing a contract for change is important for both the Child and Adult ego states of the patient. The patient must be able rationally to justify entering treatment and group therapy. Making a contract with a patient enhances the therapist's ability to bond, establish contact, and model clarity, potency, and nurturing in the later phases of treatment. The therapist informs patients of the group treatment that will follow the first session and makes them aware of the protection and nurturance available during treatment. The therapist carefully observes the overt and covert behavioral presentation made by patients and may make initial contact through wondering aloud whether they want to address their sadness, rage, physical well-being, or loneliness. The therapist will explore what patients want to change about themselves.

The change contract must be specific, reasonable, and objective. The patient must consider changes that have both behavioral and emotional consequences and that the patient, the group, and significant others can recognize. Although the Free Child in the patient may want to change, the Adapted Child may not and may fear the consequences and responsibilities of change. Thus, patients may offer to do what they will not actually do. The therapist must not agree to this type of contract. In redecision therapy, such an offer is thought of as a con and is expressed through words like "try," "want," "hope," and "can't." The therapist must listen carefully, watch the patient's behavior, and confront incongruities. The therapist may say, "Are you going to try to get a job or are you going to get one?" "Do you mean you can't stop smoking or you won't?" The redecision therapist listens carefully for the first con. The therapist confronts the con and also recognizes the possible impasse that the con represents. The therapist continues to work with the patient until they reach a contract that is within the patient's power. The contracting process is seldom finished within the first session. The patient, while working to change, will alter the treatment contract periodically.

The second session with the therapist needs to be in the group. If the therapist does further individual work with the patient, the probability of ensuing transference issues will increase. The transference may then make it more difficult for the patient to move into a group. Although the patient may have some inherent fears of entering a group, the therapist offers reassurance and provides a safe and nurturing environment that will make group entry possible. A patient's fears often grow out of a family imago (Berne, 1966b) that the patient carries and that is a representation of the family of origin. The therapist addresses the patient's fears in the intake session, if they arise, as well as in the first group session. During this first group session, the therapist is working with other patients who have been in the group for some time. The therapist and the other patients provide a model for the new patient of the way treatment will occur.

During each treatment session, the therapist will work with each patient, one at a time, for a maximum of 20 minutes. From the first session on, the therapist focuses on the patient's responsibility for the creation of his or her own bad feelings. Increased awareness of this enables the patient to be comfortable in the group. As the therapist works with other patients in the group during the session, the new patient further becomes aware of the supportive, nurturing nature of the group and of the responsibility that other patients are claiming for themselves. Also, the new patient may note that the therapist supports the capabilities of each patient and encourages feelings, behavior, and thinking. By the end of the first session, the therapist will reiterate the treatment contract with the patient to support further the changes that he or she will make. The strategy of the therapist is to follow the patient's lead and to confront the discrepancies in language and behavior that reflect where the patient is stuck. This strategy is based on the belief that the power resides within the patient and the therapist enables the patient to claim that power in a responsible way. The therapist praises the patient for attending the therapy session, for his or her willingness to talk about feelings, and for the change contract. The group may, as they choose, give positive strokes to the new patient for what they see, hear, and know of the new patient.

In redecision therapy, the therapist intervenes at an individual level in the group. The focus of this intervention is the treatment contract of the patient or what the patient wants to change about himself or herself. The therapist keeps the core of the interaction on the contract. This usually has to do with how the patient remains stuck and how the patient makes himself or herself feel bad. These matters are not often in the awareness of the patient. The therapist explores with the patient previous experiences when the patient felt bad, stuck, and unable to change personally or to alter the situation. The therapist then uses these early experiences or scenes by bringing them into the here-and-now of the group.

The therapist invites the patient to speak directly to the people in the early scene as though they are in the present and to let them know how he or she feels. The therapist coaches the patient through recreated life scenes by providing words that reflect the early decision. The patient will often find these words uncomfortable and will want to change them. The therapist then offers words that reflect a change or a redecision. The patient will either use these words or, more likely, find his or her own words that reflect a choice to change. Being in the Free Child ego state will allow the patient to correct or reframe the words.

The redecision therapist does not support or encourage interruption of the treatment process. When an interrupting patient is adamant, the therapist briefly delays work with the primary patient. Focusing momentarily on the interrupting patient, the therapist explains that patient's turn will come next and any concerns and feelings can be addressed at that time. The therapist then continues to work with the primary patient. This sort of interruption rarely occurs in redecision groups. Patients learn the manner of operation of the treatment group very early in their group experience. They know that each will have an opportunity to work on their personal contract each session. The therapist works with the interrupting patient as soon as possible and asks about feelings and beliefs at the time of the interruption. Usually, they will discover that the emotional work of the previous patient had a significant impact on this patient. Contagion plays a significant part in the redecision group. A frequent result of contagion is that each patient in the group will do some significant investigation and potentially change in relation to the feelings generated in them by other patients.

HOW REDECISION THERAPY DIFFERS

Redecision therapists address transference and countertransference in group therapy in several ways. Although the phenomena are considered important processes in the treatment experience, the therapist's strategy is to minimize their occurrence. The therapist needs to be aware of these happenings as indicators of something that may interfere with the treatment. When the patient starts to talk about strong positive or negative feelings toward the therapist, the therapist actively moves into the beliefs, feelings, and thinking of the patient. The therapist invites the patient to say the same words to various family members as though they were in the group at that moment. There is no waiting for transference feelings to develop or grow. The therapist moves the patient into an early experience or scene in which the patient had experienced those feelings and does so in the here-and-now. The patient will then either recognize how these feelings were generated and make a redecision or discover early events that have not been emotionally resolved. Either way, the patient moves along in a process of changing how he or she feels, thinks, and behaves. The activity of the redecision therapist in the treatment group minimizes the amount of transference likely to occur.

Cohesiveness of the treatment group is not seen as necessary for group treatment. As each individual experiences feelings in relation to past life events, there is an empathetic response in the group. Contagion of the strong affect of the working patient is apparent during most group sessions. This affective environment evokes in other members of the group strong feelings that are later worked with, in turn, by the therapist. By the nature of the management of feelings in the group, members are free to join with others or to limit their relatedness. The therapist, as group leader, sets and maintains clear boundaries and keeps the focus on each patient individually. That consistent focus enables the patient to use previous life scenes through being aware of the past feelings and events. The therapist views the process of focusing as a way of enabling the Child ego state of the patient to use early life decisions about feelings and behavior. The focus of the therapist on each individual enables the other patients to do silent work. Patients report many times that the most valuable gains they make come when they are "coat-tailing" on other patients' treatment. The patient, in this way, claims responsibility for the treatment and discovers the capability to empower himself or herself to change. As a group matures in time, cohesiveness develops but is not seen as either a help or a hindrance.

The patient either will or will not address the feelings and belief systems expressed in the contract for change. The patient chooses whether or not to work on the contract. The patient explores this choice, and the therapist respects it. The therapist recognizes resistance as a natural phenomenon. Each patient comes to understand that resistance is his or her own problem. With the support of the therapist, those resistant feelings can be resolved, allowing therapy to proceed at a comfortable pace. The patient learns that no one else can give him or her permission and protection to be a patient and to address those bad feelings and experiences in this way. The treatment process in redecision therapy is in the here and now. The therapist uses the patient's current experience as a vehicle for bringing relevant feelings into the present. The patient brings past, painful life experiences into the present by focusing on the bad feelings and associating to previous life scenes or events. The therapist works with the patient who is in the Child ego state and supports the awareness of the feelings and the content of the early decision. The therapist supports the patient in discovering early decisions and making new decisions. The patient's new choices are arrived at through the contract and reflect the patient's responsible use of the power to change his or her life.

An example of working from a redecision position may assist the reader in understanding this approach. This example is from a treatment group session and is taken from about midway through the session. Other patients have worked on personal issues and the group climate is both nurturing and productive of the contagion of feelings. The patient has become aware of how sad he feels through some previous work on grief by another patient.

Case Example

Patient: I've been feeling really down the past few months and I would like to do something about it. (The patient is looking sad.)

Therapist: Is this a feeling that is fairly familiar for you?

Patient: Yes, I think I have been feeling this way most of my life from time to time. Just when I think I've got it licked, it comes back.

Therapist: Tell me what "it" is.

Patient: It's the feeling that I just can't get anything done, that I'm helpless, that I feel just too tired or down or something.

Therapist: Is that what you want to change about you?

Patient: Yes.

Therapist: Will you put a word or two to that feeling?

Patient: Well, I guess, sad.

Therapist: Are you aware of feeling that now?

Patient: Yes.

Therapist: You are a little boy and you are feeling very sad and tired and down. You're aware of what's going on around you and you notice where you are.

Patient: Well, yes, and, I guess … I'm just home from school and I had just messed up on some of my schoolwork and she just isn't paying any attention to me and I'm feeling sad and she is so busy taking care of Grandma that she just ignores me.

Therapist: What are you feeling inside?

Patient: I feel real empty inside, wish she would talk to me or notice me, but she is so busy that she just isn't noticing me.

Therapist: I want you to see your mother in that empty chair and I want you to tell her how you feel.

Patient: (Patient takes several moments to prepare himself.) Mom, I sure feel bad. (Patient hesitates, begins to cry.)

Therapist: Does Mom hear you?

Patient: Mom is so busy that she just says, "Wait a minute, right now I'm busy. I'll talk to you later."

Therapist: Does Mom hear you?

Patient: No.

Therapist: Let me give you some words to say to Mom. Say to Mom, "Mom, if you won't listen to me, I'm going to feel sad the rest of my life."

Patient: I don't want to say that. That would mean that I would have to go on feeling this way forever.

Therapist: What would you rather say to her?

Patient: Mom, I am tired of feeling this way and I am not going to wait for you to notice me. You never did and you never will. I'm going to feel OK about me, no matter what you do.

Therapist: How do you feel, now that you have said that to Mom?

Patient: I don't know—I feel sort of relieved, as though a weight has been lifted. That's strange—how saying that to her would make me feel so different.

Therapist: Yes, maybe you have lifted a weight off of yourself and can now feel good, whether someone notices you or not.

This example shows how the therapist and the patient interact over the contract, how they arrive at an early scene, and how the patient resolves the bad feelings. What is missing, and difficult to describe in the example, is the therapist's awareness of the nonverbal cues that are presented by the patient. The therapist must be noting the emotional and behavioral evidence of the available Free Child ego state and the willingness of the patient to change an old decision to feel bad. The therapist must be willing for the patient not to redecide and to delay the process until the patient has had further opportunity to be aware of the choices and the risks of changing. Patients are not seen as being difficult or resistant. The redecision view is that the patient has the power to choose to change or not. The therapist stays with the patient in the Child ego state until there is a resolution of the impasse or until the patient decides not to change. A patient will make a decision not to change when there is lack of information, fear of consequences from the Parental ego state, or lack of safety. All of these the therapist will explore in later sessions with the patient. Note that, in the dialogue with the parent in the chair, the patient frames the process in the present tense and the therapist supports this interchange by keeping support also in the present tense.

The example is characteristic of a Level 2 impasse, resulting from an early decision to feel bad in a way that was modeled in the family. This type of impasse happens when important emotional messages from the Adapted Child ego state of the mother are noted by the Adapted Child of the patient. The Adapted Child ego state perceives the parent's messages as "don't" messages or injunctions. The Child ego state may interpret the meaning of the injunction and may delay or modify obedience; however, there is no awareness of an ability to disobey. In the sample, the injunction might be interpreted as meaning "Don't feel good" or "Don't be a child." Whatever the patient's Adapted Child heard, he makes a decision to obey the injunction and feel bad. The bad feeling chosen by the Adapted Child is often a bad feeling demonstrated by a significant member in the family. This impasse is often the basis of a life script.

Patients can also feel stuck in other ways. A Level 1 impasse occurs when the patient agrees with messages from the internalized Parents and continues to function in a manner that is not congruent with his or her Adult thinking. A woman who wants to improve her interchanges with her children will continue to fuss at them in spite of what she knows will work better. An example of a Level 3 impasse would be the patient who experiences a headache and is aware that he always has headaches when he is under work pressure. In this impasse, the patient feels caught in a struggle between his Free Child ego state and his Adapted Child ego state. The therapist aids the patient in resolving this impasse by having him imagine the two parts in different chairs and having them resolve their conflict with coaching from the therapist.

Impasse resolution is a mainstay for the redecision therapist in working with patients. Goulding and Goulding (1979) have provided extensive discussions of impasse resolution in their writings and give numerous examples of the three levels of impasses. Skill at impasse work comes through practice and thorough workshop supervision and training.

The redecision therapist is an active therapist. At the beginning of each session, the therapist invites group members to say what each wants to change about themselves. There are times when patients are uncertain about what they feel and think. As children, they may have heard much conflicting information about themselves, their parents, their siblings, and early life events. At such points and at other points in therapy, the therapist assists in sorting out what patients feel, think, believe, and value. TA terms this process Adult decontamination; it enables patients to discover what changes they want to make in themselves, how they want to feel, and what they want to believe. In the process, patients sometimes modify their change contracts to fit newly discovered information about themselves and their families.

A parent interview is another way for patients to discover changes they want to make in themselves. In this exercise, the therapist invites the patient to be the Parent who seems most ambiguous or vague to him or her. He then invites that Parent by given name to talk to the therapist about his or her own life, feelings, and experiences. The patient will enter that internal Parent ego state and disclose information to which the patient may not be aware he or she has access. In the Parent interview, the patient's voice, demeanor, attitude, and vocabulary change and approximate the Parent ego state from early life. The values and beliefs of that Parent also become clear. The patient is sometimes surprised at the information available through the Parent interview. Other patients in the group will corroborate for the patient the changes gone through during the process.

When a patient shows a lot of emotional distress that interferes with every-day behavior, it is vital that the therapist do "escape-hatch work." Transactional therapists believe that many patients are capable of suicide, murder, or going crazy without ever giving action to those behaviors. Even though the patient may not have serious results in mind, the potentially dangerous behavior should be confronted. If the therapist has the slightest concern that the patient may try to escape bad feelings by means of these behaviors, the therapist must work with the patient to close these escape hatches.

Escape hatches are part of the Child's early decision. They represent a way for the Child to escape or ameliorate bad feelings. To guard against these potential behaviors, at some point early in the treatment, the therapist asks patients to make a commitment to themselves. Patients are asked to say in a clear, uncomplicated fashion that they will not either accidentally or on purpose kill themselves, kill or harm anyone else, or go crazy, no matter how bad they feel and no matter how bad things get. For some clients, making these commitments is a matter of course. For others, renouncing these acts, one at a time, will often reveal hidden motives or agendas that might not otherwise surface. For these patients, there are relevant issues related to escaping bad feelings. The therapist will be given significant clues to the direction the patient may want to move in treatment. The therapist must use experience and judgment to determine whether the statements of commitment are valid and then make appropriate clinical decisions. Some patients express relief that the therapist has intervened at such a basic level and taken seriously life-threatening issues. Others experience discomfort with the therapist who confronts these concerns so directly.

CONCLUSIONS

Hundreds of therapists from all over the world have trained with the Gouldings over the years. Many more continue to train with them at Mt. Madonna. The therapists who have worked with the Gouldings have come from very different theoretical orientations and, to varying degrees, have adopted redecision philosophy and techniques. A conference of redecision therapists met at Asilomar in California in 1985 to share differing approaches to the use of the redecision therapy. The energy and vitality of the people attending that conference spoke well for the approach. The appearance of redecision therapists at many other conferences and professional meetings also demonstrates continuing interest in the approach. Attendance at workshops in which the philosophy and techniques are being taught is further evidence.

There is a small but growing body of research literature on redecision therapy, beginning with the report on encounter groups in the book by Lieberman, Yalom, and Miles (1973). It was through that study that the basic stance of the therapist for group management in redecision was reported. Robert L. Goulding was known to be one of the most successful leaders in that study. To quote from Paul McCormick's (1978) review of the study:

> The researchers studied the characteristics of the most successful group leaders and found that they had the following in common: (a) they were only moderate in their use of "emotional stimulation" (they did not seduce the clients with charisma); (b) they rated high in "caring"; (c) they stressed "meaning attribution" (they offered explanations of what they observed, and information on how to change); and (d) they were only moderate in "executive function" (their use of structured exercises, and of "group management"). The method of treatment (whether psychoanalytic, gestaltist, psychodramatic, etc.) was less significant than the characteristics of the treaters. (p. ii)

These are the characteristics that the Gouldings demonstrate and model in all of their training workshops.

The structure and theory of redecision therapy lend themselves to fulfilling current needs for short-term treatment groups. The effectiveness of this approach on a wide range of psychological problems has not been well studied or tested. This could be done with reasonable ease, given the use of objective treatment contracts and the measurability of the changes that the patient desires. Current efforts by health-care programs to limit psychological treatment could be fulfilled by judicious use of redecision therapy. Contracts for treatment would be easily understood and results related to the treatment contract. Although it could not be posited that this treatment approach would take less time, the costs of group treatment versus individual therapy would be significant.

Redecision therapy does not make use of and, therefore, does not fit well with the psychological nomenclature found in current diagnostic and statistical manuals. Using a Raschian model for human distress as described by Wiggins (1980), the prototypic nature of treatment contracts would permit systematic study of this treatment approach. This model, influenced by circumplex models and nonderogatory classifications, would lend itself to both more humane and more relevant psychological treatment.

REFERENCES

Berne, E. (1961). *Transactional analysis in psychotherapy.* New York: Grove.

Berne, E. (1966a). *The structure and dynamics of organizations and groups.* Philadelphia: Lippincott.

Berne, E. (1966b). *Principles of group treatment.* New York: Grove.

Berne, E. (1972). *What do you say after you say hello?* New York: Grove.

Gladfelter, J. H. (1977). Enjoying every minute. In G. Barnes (Ed.), *Transactional analysis after Eric Berne* (pp. 384–424). New York: Harper's College Press.

Gladfelter, J. H. (1990). Integrated psychotherapy. In J. K. Zeig & W. M. Munion (Eds.), *What is psychotherapy?* (pp. 336–340). San Francisco: Jossey/Bass.

Goulding, M., & Goulding, R. (1979). *Changing lives through redecision therapy.* New York: Brunner/Mazel.

Goulding, R. L. (1977). No magic at Mt. Madonna: Redecisions in Marathon Therapy. In G. Barnes (Ed.), *Transactional analysis after Eric Berne* (pp. 77–98). New York: Harper's College Press.

Goulding, R. L., & Goulding, M. M. (1978). *The power is in the patient.* San Francisco: TA Press.

Kadis, L. (1985). *Redecision therapy: Expanded perspectives.* Watsonville, CA: Western Institute.

Lieberman, M. A., Yalom, L. D., & Miles, M. B. (1973). *Encounter groups: First facts.* New York: Basic Books.

McCormick, P. (1978). Editor's preface. In M. Goulding & R. Goulding, *The power is in the patient.* San Francisco: TA Press.

McNeel, J. R. (1977). The seven components of redecision therapy. In G. Barnes (Ed.), *Transactional analysis after Eric Berne.* New York: Harper's College Press.

Perls, F. (1969). *Gestalt therapy verbatim.* Lafayette, CA: Real People Press.

Stern, D. (1985). *The interpersonal world of the infant.* New York: Basic Books.

Stewart, I., & Joines, V. S. (1987). *TA Today.* Nottingham & Chapel Hill: Lifespace Publishing.

Wiggins, J. S. (1980). Circumplex models of interpersonal behavior. In L. Wheeler (Ed.), *Review of personality and social psychology* (Vol. 1). Beverly Hills: Sage.

CHAPTER 16

Transactional Analysis in Groups*

JOHN J. O'HEARNE

I was surprised the other day when Jeff, a very intact 35-year-old friend, confided in me that, as a youngster, he had a lot of group therapy.

Jeff said: "From about age 10 to 15, I was intermittently in therapy groups. My folks were a squabbling, alcoholic pair. Being in a group meant I not only got to talk about my own disorderly life but also to learn about others' pain. I found I was neither unusual nor alone."

INTRODUCTION

Transactional analysis (TA) is a psychological theory and the method of treatment that follows from that theory. It was originated by Eric Berne, a psychiatrist who had studied at McGill University when the neurosurgeon Wilder Penfield was discovering there that, if he stimulated discrete areas of the brain with a fine enough electrode, he could elicit entire memories, not just sensations. Berne had also studied psychoanalysis for 13 years at the New York Psychoanalytic Institute and the San Francisco Psychoanalytic Institute. During the latter part of that training, he published his first paper on transactional analysis (Berne, 1958).

TA theory lacks two major theories that need to be borrowed from psychoanalysis: working through and oedipal situations. It may be used with individual patients, couples, families, and large groups, such as business institutions, churches, and schools. It has one further advantage: much of the work in TA can be done in a way that is fun and efficient for both the patient and the therapist.

---

* Reprinted with permission from O'Hearne, J. (1993). Transactional analysis in groups. In H.I. Kaplan and B.J. Sadock (Eds.) Comprehensive group psychotherapy (3rd ed., pp. 205–214). Lippincott Williams and Wilkins.

THEORY

Ego States

Berne documented the beginning of his thoughts about ego states when he truly listened to one of his patients, a young attorney. The man showed Berne that he functioned in two different states: one, the successful, professional man; the other, a young boy. Sometimes, the man would say to Berne, "Are you talking to the lawyer or to the little boy?"

After reflection on that question, Berne conceptualized what he called *ego states*. To the original Child and Adult ego states, Berne later added the third ego state, Parent. The basic concepts of TA began with those three ego states. They refer to the idea that a person who has those three major states and is an autonomous person shifts flexibly and appropriately from one state to another. If the words "parent," "adult," and "child" are written in lower case, they carry their ordinary meanings. When they are capitalized in transactional analysis, they refer to ego states. Those ego states are represented as three circles, superimposed, with the Parent the top circle and the Child the bottom circle (Figure 1).

The neurosurgical work of Penfield in eliciting discrete memories by localized stimulation of the brain may have influenced Berne in recognizing that those three major states of being are within one person.

TA therapists are fond of saying that id, ego, and superego are philosophical constructs but that ego states are existential realities, externally observable. Berne's (1961) definition of ego states as "coherent systems of thoughts, feelings, and behavior patterns" is not precise enough for many students. The con-

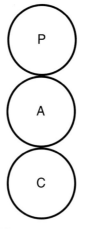

FIGURE 1   Ego States

cept is difficult to define satisfactorily in words. It is much easier to demonstrate in action.

A young man was undergoing psychiatric evaluation after holding up a convenience store with the type of gun used to start swim meets. The gun shoots only blanks. He said that he did not know why he held up the store, nor why he stopped when the traffic light turned red against him after he left the store. The therapist taught him the principles of ego states and then asked the same questions. At first, the young man said that he did not know why he robbed the store. The therapist said: "I'm not talking to that grown-up part of you. I'm talking to the little boy. How was it to have the gun in your pocket, approaching the store?" The man said with a smile, "Exciting." He was asked again how he felt when he pointed the gun at the manager. Smiling once again, he said, "That was real exciting." The therapist said, "Did you consider that he might have a real gun with real bullets?" The young man's face turned white, and he said, "I could have gotten killed!"

The TA way of looking at that is to say that the Adult state did not know why he robbed the store. Obviously, the Child part of him did. That example illustrates the youth of the Child ego state, which is usually thought of as being no older than 8 years. When asked if he had thought that the manager might have a real gun with real bullets, the patient shifted into the Adult ego state and realized the danger of what he had done. He was a good Child when he obeyed the traffic light. Specifically, he was in his Adapted Child, a functional division of the Child state. By the time children are 8 years of age, they have almost always adapted to the desires of the important powerful people in their world. That adaptation influences them for the rest of their lives, whether it is a healthy adaptation or not. The other functional division of the Child is the Natural (sometimes called Free) Child. That is the Child as it was before adaptation. Under the influence of continuing messages from the Parent, the Adapted Child may try to disown or to overpower the Natural Child.

The Parent ego state is originally recorded like a videotape in the brain. Much of it is recorded by sight, sound, and feelings. Only later do the words register. The primary functions of the Parent are functionally subdivided into Nurturing Parent and Critical Parent. The Nurturing Parent comforts, guides, soothes, and sustains. It has both positively and negatively valued sets of functions. For example, if the nurturing is overdone, it is not-OK parenting that is likely to influence the child *not* to grow up. The positive side helps the child grow up autonomously. The Critical Parent, on its positive side, limits the child with appropriate warnings and discipline, such as, "Don't touch the stove!" The negative, not-OK aspect of that functional subdivision is destructive criticism. Those functional subdivisions are represented in Figure 2.

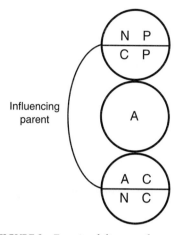

FIGURE 2   Functional diagram of ego states.

Diagnosis   Ego states are diagnosable by words and such nonverbal communications as voice tone, posture, gesture, facial expression, proxemics, and kinesics. If a Parent sharply criticizes the Child, the Child may literally cringe and curl up into a small ball, cry, and whine, "I can't." Such quick diagnosis can be taught to patients, groups, and families. But many beginning TA therapists are likely to overuse the simplicity of the method, resulting in jargon.

When the present author first read Berne's 1958 paper, he slammed the book shut with disgust and left the library. He had spent many thousands of dollars in his own psychoanalysis and supervision. It seemed an insult to believe that human personality could be roughly diagrammed with three circles. Later, when he introduced the concepts of TA to the Japanese Psychosomatic Society, he was told there that the word "transaction" did not translate well into Japanese, since transactions are for the field of business, not family relationships. His hosts tried to translate it with a concept they termed "mutually yielding–mutually influencing." That term fits nicely with modern systems theory and emphasizes TA's stress on the interpersonal.

To read Berne's (1964) best-known book, *Games People Play*, is to struggle through what Berne intended to be an encyclopedia. There, he tried to explain complex phenomena in simple words, and his pedantry detracts from the simplicity. Seeing TA in operation, as on a videotape of a therapy session, and thus learning the basic concepts in action is a much easier way to learn TA than by reading a few books. The required book learning follows more easily after one is shown the concepts in action. That emphasis on observable data reduces regression in therapy and makes it easy for the principles of TA to be taught to many people, including children.

That simplicity and ease, along with the usefulness of influencing others to shift ego states, led to customer-contact training programs in industries, such as major airlines and banks, in churches, and for many mental health professionals (Morrison & O'Hearne, 1977). Of course, much more is involved in using TA as a method of psychotherapy than influencing people to change ego states. Its usefulness is recognized in the specialized training that the American Group Psychotherapy Association has provided at their annual conferences and in clinical courses given at annual meetings of the American Psychiatric Association.

Therapy

In psychotherapy, TA insists on an intact, well-functioning Adult ego state. That first order of business has multilayered importance. It is necessary for an adequate treatment contract to be made, and it is important that, when leaks or contaminations occur, they be healed. By so doing, patients do not speak opinion (a Parent function) when they believe they are speaking fact. For example, a borderline personality disorder may have leaks between all three ego states and between the Adult state and the outside world. An ego state diagram of a patient suffering from a severe borderline personality disorder may show leaks or contaminations as illustrated in Figure 3. (The customary TA teaching shows such contaminations by overlapping the ego states. The author prefers to think of them as leaks between membranes that have become more than semipermeable. That use makes clear the need to seal the leak by distinguishing fact from feeling.)

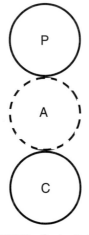

FIGURE 3   Contamination.

The word "transactional" refers to the transactions or moves that people make in their dealings with each other. An important communication theory principle is demonstrated in work with transactions. If a speaker addresses a particular ego state in the other person and that ego state responds, communication between them can proceed smoothly. If, however, the addressed ego state does not respond but another one does, the crossed transaction necessitates the two persons moving back to complementary transactions or remaining at the level of the crossed transaction like two sword-fighters whose swords are crossed. In the latter case, they may agree to disagree (Berne, 1961).

Games

"Games" does not refer to fun and games, since in psychological games people may die. Unfortunately for many of his followers, Berne chose the term "game." He noted that the moves or transactions between people often resemble those of a zero-sum game like football. In a psychological game, transactions seem to be going smoothly until a cross and surprise ending results in bad feelings for one, maybe both, of the participants. Those bad feelings may range from a mild discomfort to literal death, as in the game of Rapo (Berne, 1964).

The group in which Berne formulated his early ideas of games was a group of couples whom he thought he could not hurt, since they were not benefiting efficiently from their therapy. He assembled them into a group and there noticed that each member of a couple blamed the other partner for their troubles. Then, he noted that many other people in partnerships did the same thing. He termed that game If It Weren't for You. He soon discovered that at least one of the partners, often both, used phobic mechanisms to avoid anxiety. The finding that both members of the couple were involved in phobic behavior contrasted with the belief that phobias are intrapsychic phenomena involving only one person, who has the disease. That finding was behind Berne's formulating the concept of games and in teaching ways to stop such destructive behavior and to help patients become healthy, become winners. Winners make good on their own contracts with themselves (James, 1977).

One of the most helpful contributions from TA to the group psychotherapist concerns the question "How do people spend their time?" Berne (1964) and Muriel James (1977) listed six ways: withdrawal, ritual, pastime, activity, game, and intimacy. A seventh has since been added: play.

Beginning group psychotherapists may be uncomfortable when patients are pastiming, discussing news, markets, prices, entertainment, for example The therapists may stir up unnecessary, unfruitful feelings by insisting that the group get down to work. Similar lulls may occur after an especially dramatic breakthrough by a patient or by the group as a whole.

Strokes

As the ego states are the anatomy of TA, so are strokes the physiology. So felic-
itous is the underlying idea that the word "stroke" has already become part of
everyday North American speech. A stroke is originally a biological stimulus
to the infant, such as stroking the baby's skin or rocking it. With maturation,
that original biological stimulus may become a social stimulus, a unit of
recognition, such as a student's making eye contact with a lecturer, a smile, a
nod, a gold watch at a retirement ceremony. The concept is especially well
detailed in an early popularization of TA, *Born to Win* (James & Jongeward,
1971). Spitz (1945), in his studies on hospitalism, showed the necessity for
frequent and favorable biological and social contact between the infant and
the caretaker. Sensory-deprivation experiments show how rapidly adults
begin to lose contact with the world and begin to be psychotic. If the group
therapist is aware that humans are mammals and that all mammals affiliate in
infancy or die, it should not be surprising that people continually balance
their need and desire for strokes between desire-impulse and what they perceive as taboo or unwise.

Group psychotherapists have their own rules concerning touch. The following are some of the questions that present themselves in most groups: "If
patients are sad, may or should I touch them? Hold one of their hands? Put an
arm around them? Will all touch lead to sexual acting out? Do I, as a therapist,
treat alike patients who come from touch cultures and those from nontouch
cultures? If a patient asks for a hug, what do I do? Can patients contract to be
held for a definite number of minutes as a regular part of their therapy? Will I
hug in group therapy but not in individual therapy?"

If the therapist is convinced that such touching is wrong—for example, if
it is thought to be countertransferential or seductive or if the patient has
conned the therapist through helplessness—it definitely should not be done.
The intent of the therapist's message through touching cannot be determined
until the patient responds, since the message intended and the message actually sent may or may not be received the way the sender intended. As Birdwhistell (1963) wrote: "Meaning is not immanent in particular symbols,
words, sentences or acts of whatever duration but in the behavior elicited by
the *presence or absence of such behavior* in particular contexts." (The italics
are Birdwhistell's.)

A beautiful young woman with an inoperable sarcoma had just returned from
the first of many visits she would make to a distant cancer treatment center. She
was seated next to the therapist. She began the group session by entertaining the
other members, telling them of the consternation she started in the hospital's
admission area. When she and her mother had waited more than an hour, she
sat on a wheeled examining stool and scooted around the floor. (That was an

Adult use of the Child state. She knew they would get attention sooner that way. She was right.) Then she quickly changed and looked angry. Her chin was defiantly poised, her forehead was furrowed in anger, her voice was harsh as she said that she refused chemotherapy because she would lose all her hair. The therapist took her arm, raised it as though proclaiming a winner, and said, "The champ." She instantly relaxed and laughed, then told the rest of the story. Similar verbal and nonverbal stroking for her chosen ego state, a defiant Adapted Child, was helpful through the entire course of her illness (O'Hearne, 1981).

Supportive therapy in TA includes, first, clarifying the boundaries of the Adult ego state and then stroking the patient's preferred ego state action. Other activities may also be needed—for example, resocialization and environmental manipulation. The therapist invites or induces the patient to shift to the appropriate ego state. Here, it is especially important to stroke the Adapted Child, as in the example above. That need not be done in a boringly serious way. TA therapists are often most comfortable when being spontaneous. The majority of them live out Grotjahn's (1983) desideratum: "The group therapist is nothing if he is not spontaneous. He depends on his immediate, intuitive, emotional, and honest responses.... The group therapist may make mistakes; he is expected and allowed to do so."

In his second group session, a new man sat stiffly erect and stonefaced. When he frowned at the therapist, the therapist imitated his posture and his frown. The man relaxed partially and said, "I thought we were here to work on our problems."

The therapist countered, "Work on them so efficiently that they are no longer bothersome."

The new man continued: "Seems to me that most of the first session and today are more like play than work. I'm ready to go to work on mine."

The therapist said, "And with your willingness to be serious when it is appropriate and to work, you've got a wonderful prospect of reaching the goals you and I set together."

The man relaxed, and a woman asked him in a perfectly serious Adult manner, "Do you have fun or just work?"

In a very serious manner, he replied: "I do have *some* fun. But not much really. I'm always thinking or working."

A few group members laughed, and the therapist stroked his Adapted Child again by saying: "There's always plenty to think about and to notice and to work on. If you feel uncomfortable here and people try to make you become lighthearted overnight, you don't need to give in to it. Your seriousness and thoughtfulness and willingness to work have served you well so far."

In so doing, the therapist realized that he was approving the patient's Adapted State and that the patient's internalized Parent was far less likely to obstruct his next steps in growth.

Contracts

Much TA literature gives the impression that almost all TA therapists start treatment with a tight treatment contract. That is true only in some cases. In other cases, it may be far more helpful to form a relationship that includes trust and a good working relationship and then to clarify the treatment contract (O'Hearne, 1976; James, 1977). In the area of contract formation lies a significant difference from the contract in psychoanalytic therapy. In TA, the contract is often more explicit than in psychoanalytic therapy. A soft contract would be "To improve my social skills." In connection with such a vague contract, Berne is reputed to have said that, if the pilot announced before takeoff from San Francisco that he would try to take them toward New York, Eric would want off the airplane. A harder, more explicit contract includes specific and measurable goals, such as, "When I have not been late for work a single time in three consecutive months, I'll be ready to stop coming." Before the end of three months, the patient may want to revise the contract. The therapist checks the fulfillment of the first contract before accepting the revision.

The most important contract a patient can make is a no-suicide contract. An experienced therapist can help patients make that explicit contract with themselves: "No matter what happens, no matter how I feel, I will not kill myself, either accidentally or on purpose" (Drye, Goulding, & Goulding, 1973). Clinical judgment must be exercised here. The therapist should not feel confident merely because the patient agrees to the words. The words are not magic. However, the skilled use of the contract has enabled many patients to avoid hospitalization. Sometimes, patients agree to keep the agreement only until a certain date. If that is the case, the therapist must carefully review the decision before the expiration date.

A 32-year-old woman made a no-suicide contract for an indefinite period. Her clinical condition deteriorated until the day she came for her individual appointment, showed obvious depression, and said, "I can no longer honor that contract. I don't believe I slept at all last night. All I can think of is killing myself. It's all so useless. You and I had agreed that, if I ever thought I could no longer honor the contract, I'd talk it over with you face-to-face."

The therapist verified her helpless, hopeless, depressed attitude and told her that she would need to be hospitalized, since she was having too much difficulty in keeping her head above water, that even hope was dying.

She nodded assent.

He called the hospital, then said, "Let's go. To the hospital." She said, "Can't I go home to get a nightie and toothbrush?" The therapist sternly said, "'Those aren't necessary yet. Your safety is. We can get someone to bring them to you. Let's go."

As she improved in the hospital, she told her physician, "I'd be dead if I hadn't kept that contract. I remembered that I had decided, when I was still young, that I would not live past 33. And the day I had to come to the hospital was my 33rd birthday. I'd forgotten that."

Few suicidal patients have had anyone forbid them to kill themselves. TA teaches the importance of powerfully commanding them not to kill themselves, because no one can help them when they are dead; suicide is a permanent solution to a temporary problem. The command must come from the Parent in the therapist, who must speak more powerfully than the Parent that the patient has recorded in the brain. It must then be followed with Adult fact: No one can help you when you are dead. The author has had three patients with no-suicide contracts who came close to killing themselves. All three stopped when they "heard" his voice, commanding them not to kill themselves. They knew that no one else could have heard the voice, but, as soon as they heard it, they stopped flirting with suicide and called for emergency appointments.

Case Example

A 31-year-old man was referred by his internist because "he has kept so much in that he's getting ready to blow" and "he's so tense that his muscles are beginning to ache." The internist thought the patient needed psychotherapy more than simply muscle relaxers.

The man's face was like a mask, showing fear, grim determination, and anger. His gaze was hyperalert; he could move very quickly. He reminded the therapist of a spring that had been wound too tight.

He was the first-born child, followed by a brother and two sisters. He described his mother in vague terms; he described his father as mean and impulsive, the boss of the home and of the family business. As the boys matured, the father began driving as much as 1000 miles a weekend to pursue his hobby of racing cars, and he took the boys. When the patient was 10 years of age, his father would have the boy help him by watching while the father worked on engines, sometimes trying to guess which tools the father wanted and having them ready for him. If the guess was wrong, his father would berate and sometimes slap him. The patient remembered deciding, before he was 12, that he could never please his father, and yet he wanted to be with him, so he learned to stay just beyond his reach and to move quickly. His mother never protected him from his father.

In individual therapy, the therapist taught the patient the theory of ego states. The patient could then see that it was an Adult fact that his father's actions were not proper fatherly behavior and that other fathers did not behave similarly. Yet, the patient sometimes felt that something must be wrong with him, since his father did not attack the younger son nearly as much. That small contamination was readily cured when the patient realized that his worth did not depend on what his father did with his little brother. The patient admitted that his Natural Child was very small and locked in except when he drove out of town with several close male friends. He could see that other men his age usually went out with women, and he reminded the therapist that he had some growing up to do before going out with girls. He had adapted by locking in many aggressive feelings and the desire for esteem, closeness, and touch. He said he was fairly clear about himself and knew that he was locked in and had missed a lot and that he did not know much about normal people and how they lived.

The therapist replied: "I agree. You have just written the prescription for the best form of therapy for you—group therapy. There, you can see how other people live and how they have adapted. You have adapted so well that you could continue to get by, but you've already seen the price you must pay for your false feeling of safety. True, staying locked in and on guard can keep you out of your father's range, but it does nothing to cure the relationship between you and Dad. It deprives you of most fun, all romance, and most love."

The patient knew he would be uncomfortable in the therapy group and wondered what he would do there. The therapist had him agree to (1) keep confidential the identity of the others in the group, (2) not hit anyone present and not damage the therapist's office, and (3) not have sex with anyone in the group. Then, the therapist told the patient that he could just watch the first time and that he could talk whenever he wanted, but he would have to do what people did in normal families—that is, compete for airtime.

The therapist deliberately did not make a tight treatment contract, because he believed that the man's treatment would not be along the lines of a medical model but would be humanistic.

In his first group session, the man sat erect, eyes and head moving freely and rapidly as the focus changed from one patient to another. He did not look scared, but he still looked tight. His facial expression barely changed during the 90 minutes. The therapist did not ordinarily see a group patient between the first two group sessions, to prevent the patient's remaining inactive and holding all the tensions for the work in individual therapy.

In the second group session, the man's behavior was much the same, including his inscrutable facial expression. Berne (1966) had taught that it is part of the group therapist's job to help each patient differentiate from the others present, just as should have been done in the family of origin (Bowen, 1978). Accordingly, toward the end of the second session, the therapist asked the man if he wanted to say anything. He did not.

In the next individual session, the therapist reviewed the patient's behaviors. The patient smiled gently and said he still did not feel like saying anything in the group. The therapist asked if he could see how the group could be useful to him.

The patient replied, "That and these times I have with you. I am already see-ing how different my family was and is from most other families."

His pattern of not speaking in the group continued; other members finally asked so many questions about him that he started telling them about his work. For the first time, so far as he could remember, people were enjoying his accounts of his success. They smiled when he told of the top boss's asking him to do something that, normally, the firstline manager should have done. Before long, he was asked to become a manager in training. The group celebrated that achievement with him, and he smiled broadly. In individual therapy, he said that he did not feel comfortable telling them about what happened in his fam-ily of origin; he would not feel right. That feeling was analyzed as reluctance and fear of breaking the family's code and his feeling uneasy that the other members might think he was too odd to be around. That leak between the Child and Adult ego states was healed by showing him that that had not been his experience in the group when others told about their origins. In subse-quent group sessions, the patient told the group about his family. Some of the women—when they heard of his father's slapping him, cursing him, and ridi-culing him at the family table and in public—were angry. The therapist asked if the man was surprised at that reaction. He was. Did he have any evidence that his mother had any feelings at all when that was going on?

In the next individual session, the patient began to speak of his recent efforts to get his mother to see his side. She would not, and she said such things as, "He's not that way all the time."

In the next group session, the patient started telling about trying to get his mother to see his side and to give him some backing against Dad at home. At that point, another man started to advise him what he should do with both parents. A woman in the group said angrily to that man: "He doesn't need your help. He's doing fine on his own. Your own son cut you off because of your constant advising. That doesn't help you or your son!"

The other man's contract included becoming aware of how often he com-pulsively tried to help others by playing the game I'm Only Trying to Help You. That is the most common game played by therapists. In it, the person offers help, compulsively, without being asked. Such behavior can be thought of as a game in which the helper proves his superiority over the helpless person. Bad feelings occur when the helpless one commonly wins the round by reverting to Yes, But, which tells the helper why the suggestion will not work; thus, the helpless one wins a round. I'm Only Trying to Help You is a manifestation of a reaction formation against the helper's own dependent needs.

The helper in the group looked hurt and ready to argue. The therapist con-tinued with the previously frozen man, saying, "Did you ever see your mother defend you against your father like that?"

The patient said, "No."

The therapist asked, "They didn't argue over which one of them was right in their opinions about how to rear children?"

The patient said: "Never that I remember. I'm trying to get her to wake up now. It's still going on at home, and I've got sisters and a brother who are all about to leave home."

The therapist turned to the woman and the man who had just shown the patient a world he had never known. He asked them how they had felt as the formerly frozen man was talking, saying, "It must have been very important for both you, since you both cared enough to send your very best."

Each told of home backgrounds that were isomorphically similar to the formerly frozen man's background. Each felt helpless rage at someone else's being treated in ways similar to the ways their families lived.

The therapist believed that the focus needed to shift away from the frozen man, so that he could integrate how he felt when two people he regarded as more mature than he also felt strongly about his plight. Accordingly, the therapist shifted to the helper man and reminded him that his contract called for him to become aware how often he volunteered help before anyone asked for it. That man denied that he was doing that, and the majority of the group members told him he had been at it again. The helper felt hurt, and the therapist stroked him, complimenting him for caring, sending his very best, yet offering help when it was not asked. The helper pouted that he was just ... and the therapist intervened, "There's nothing wrong with helping others except when it keeps us from knowing you, knowing how much you wish your Dad had protected you against your mother's chronic criticism of you, knowing how small you felt when you realized again and again that you could never please her."

The helper got tears in his eyes and looked hurt.

The therapist asked, "Remember what you felt like back then?" The helper said he surely did.

The therapist said: "While you are sitting here, go on back there to those bad feelings. You can handle them now. We're all here with you."

Soon, that big man started talking about how life was way back then. The therapist asked him to live it through, to tell it in the present tense. As the helper did, he used some Child language, cried gently, and said, "I never can please you."

The therapist asked, "Can anybody please her?"

The man said, "No."

The therapist said, "Then tell her so."

The man did so, quietly.

To increase his affective investment in the scene, the therapist said, "Maybe she tuned you out. Tell her real loud."

Instead, the man cried gently.

The therapist said, "You have plenty to feel sad about. You never will be able to please your Mommie. She is unhappy most of the time, and neither you nor your Dad can please her, no matter what you do. You can be the goodest boy in the school, and you can't please her. Come on back up to today, and tell her that you understand now why you couldn't make her happy then. She had something wrong with her. It wasn't you."

The therapist threw a cushion on the floor, had the patient let it be a stand-in for his mother, and coached him in increasing his Adult strength in the redecision, based on Adult awareness, not compulsive repetition of his original childhood fixation.

Techniques

The redecision method of treatment has been popularized by Goulding and Goulding (1978, 1979) and has been taught to thousands of therapists worldwide. For many TA therapists, redecision approaches have supplanted Berne's classic method, in which a potent therapist commands the patient to live healthily, thus disobeying the internalized Parent, and then gives Adult reasons to do so. Such a therapist must anticipate that the patient's Parent will put up a hard fight and must be ready to protect the patient from such an onslaught—for example, by saying: "And if that witch scares you against changing to such extent that you are too uncomfortable, you may call me. But now that you understand what's going on, it probably won't be necessary."

The author finds both methods useful, with the classic method often being quicker to use in an emergency. The classic method allows the patient to temporarily regress in the service of the ego. Such regression is much more limited in the redecision model, in which the patient cathects the Child state, reexperiences the repeated trauma in that state, and is then asked to return to the present, where the Adult ego state is used to drop the early decision, made by a child with child-level information, and to adopt an Adult redecision, based on grown-up information. Groups may cheer at the redecision, thus strengthening it.

The author expects either or both of two behaviors in the next group or individual therapy sessions: (1) acceptance and working through of grief at the level of a child, realizing that the dream is gone, that the patient does not have the power to make the parents happy; such working through is often neglected in TA (O'Hearne, 1981); (2) grief in the patient's Nurturing Parent. The reframing (Bandler & Grinder, 1982) suddenly shifts the patient's Gestalt. Instead of the original parent as an unpleasable ogre, the patient's Parent feels sad at the inability to help the parent. That grief also needs working through, since it involves a final acceptance of the fact that the parent may die, unchanged and unhappy. If patients are not in profound grief at that point, the author may ask, "If your parent died today, how do you believe you'd feel when they closed the lid on the casket?" That question sharply confronts the patient with reality in the grown-up world. Then, the author may ask: "Do you believe it is now possible to do anything about the relationship you have with that parent? If so, what? If you are going to do anything about it, when will you do it?"

Use with Other Techniques

TA marries well with Gestalt orientations and with Bowenian theses. If patients have disturbed relations in their present lives, the therapist urges them to go back and fix them in their families of origin, if possible. Most major modern approaches for psychotherapy can be used with TA, except for one that uses regressive transferences in treatment. One orientation that does not fit with TA are the encounter techniques of yelling at an empty chair that represents an original frustrator for the patient. Yelling in anger over and over again is not compatible with TA. TA knows that patients must be in an Adult ego state when leaving a therapy session so that they are capable of going safely on their way.

Script Analysis

Script analysis is what is necessary for a lasting cure in many people. "Although people are not usually aware of it, their psychological scripts, like those of stage plays, contain not only the themes, but also the roles they expect to play, the roles they expect others to play, the dramatic action, climax, and denouement" (James, 1977). The central plot is usually decided early in life, and how to make it happen is usually decided during adolescence. The plot can usually be expressed in such words as "never," "always," "almost," and "after." Useful questions to consider are "Would this be the script for a comedy, a tragedy, a bore, or a soap opera? Does the central character present as a victim, a rescuer, or a persecutor? Which myths follow the same plot, and how do they end?" A typical script matrix of a person similar to the helper described above is given in Figure 4.

The Child state of the helper's mother gave the injunction that negated normal healthy growth. It can best be understood if that Child state of the mother is regarded as only 2 years older than the patient. That is a major advantage in TA; patients must recognize that their parents were children, too. The Adult fact is that no parent ever does it all right. The Child state in the patient's mother conveyed a message to the developing child that can be summarized as "Don't be happy." His father's Child did not give a countervailing early message. The patient's father did show him how to do man's work and how to obey his mother's injunction by trying to cheer her up, anticipate her needs, excuse her complaining, and help the neighbors. The Parent part of his parents taught him values he could repeat to any Sunday School class: Be good, kind, patient, and help others.

Educating people about their scripts is similar to a psychoanalyst's explaining the oedipal situation to patients, so that they do not need to analyze it. Redecision as described above and by Goulding and Goulding (1978, 1979) is the most commonly used method in TA.

Other Techniques

Not all methods work in the hands of all therapists for all people, so it is well to know other ways, such as working through (O'Hearne, 1981) and the self-reparenting techniques of Muriel James (1981).

Self-reparenting is not to be confused with reparenting, a technique involving massive regression, with all the risks that can entail for patients who turn over much of the control of their lives to therapists who seem to believe that they can cure such severe illnesses such as schizophrenia by such methods. James's self-reparenting is safe because it is self-limited. It need not be confined to very sick people. It includes having the patients express clearly what they wish they had heard and experienced at important times early in their lives. Some of the things they wish they had heard can be read from their lists by other people in the workshop or the therapy group.

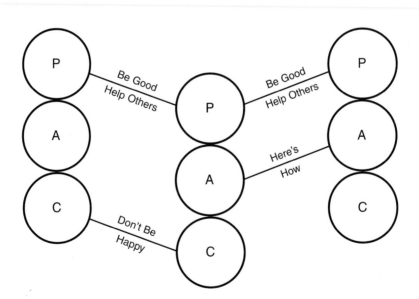

FIGURE 4   Script matrix.

The author believes in the necessity of working through necessary grief as a means of cementing the changes that usually occur when powerful treatment methods are used. Such working through is not always necessary, especially when the therapy is done in a marathon therapy session (usually two days, at least). If the patients show decreased mobility, a slow rate of speech, and other bodily symptoms and signs consistent with dysphoria or depression, they can usually do important working through in two or three sessions.

Termination

Termination may be considered in the first consultation by asking such questions as, "What is the least amount of change you will accept?" How will we know when you have reached your goal? How will you be seen differently then by those who know you best? Who will object to your changing? How will you tend to sabotage your changing? Who will benefit from your changing?" Those questions focus on the interpersonal field, in contrast to the intrapsychic world. When the patient talks of leaving therapy, the therapist should check the contract made at the beginning, along with any amendments. The patients must believe that they can check their progress; they can even make a road map of it, checking the progress markers they have established. Doing so reduces regression and makes for a quickly efficient working relationship.

Training

When first encountered, the basic principles of TA seem intriguingly simple. The basic principles *are* simple. Merely making patients aware of their maladaptive behavior and guarding against its expression is helpful social control and usually reduces symptoms quickly. Some of the other concepts—such as script analysis; changing a patient's basic existential stance; the second-by-second miniscript work of Taibi Kahler and Hedges Capers (1974), which allows people to become aware of how they are influencing, in seconds to minutes, their own behavior—are more difficult than the basic principles. Berne insisted that people joining the International Transactional Analysis Association be licensable in their own healing professions, be grounded in basic clinical sciences, and understand child development, including the developmental schemata of Erik Erikson. The members of the association set up standards of training and clinical examinations for prospective clinical members. Those examinations covered both theory and its application, as judged in audiotaped samples of the applicant's therapeutic work. Applicants seeking advanced status as training members were required to know advanced theory, bring tapes of some of their teaching sessions, and teach students at the examination site. The demand was made to admit people who do not have degrees in clinical skills into membership. When the governing board allowed it, the organization grew rapidly from the eight original students at the San Francisco Social Psychiatry Seminar of 1958 into an international organization with more than 11,000 members.

The author has found that a 200-hour training course is usually sufficient for trained psychotherapists to become comfortable with applying TA in their clinical practices. He has found that marathon therapy sessions of several days, with ample sleep time to avoid undesired regression, are usually sufficient to introduce people to TA, to provide an effective stimulus for the resumption of growth in patients being treated with any form of psychotherapy when it is temporarily stalled, and for the treatment of many problems presented by couples.

REFERENCES

Bandler, R., & Grinder, J. (1982). *Reframing.* Moab, Utah: Real People Press.

Berne E. (1966). *Structure and dynamics of organizations and groups.* New York: Oxford Univ. Press.

Berne E. (1964). *Games people play.* New York: Grove Press.

Berne E. (1961). *Transactional analysis in psychotherapy.* New York: Grove Press.

Berne E. (1958). Transactional analysis: A new and effective method of group psychotherapy. *American Journal of Psychopathy, 12,* 735.

Birdwhistell, R. (1963). Research in the structure of group psychotherapy. *Journal of Group Psychotherapy, 13,* 485.

Bowen, M. (1978). *Family therapy in clinical practice.* New York: Aronson.

Dies, R. (1992). Models of group therapy: Sifting through confusion. *International Journal of Group Psychotherapy, 42,* 1.

Drye, R., Goulding, R., & Goulding, M. (1973). No-suicide decision: Patient monitoring of suicidal risk. *American Journal of Psychiatry, 130,* 171.

Gladfelter J. (1992). Redecision therapy. *International Journal of Group Psychotherapy, 42,* 319.

Goulding, M., & Goulding, R. (1979). *Changing lives through therapy.* New York: Brunner/Mazel.

Goulding, R., & Goulding, M. (1978). *The power is in the patient.* San Francisco: TA Press.

Grotjahn M. (1983.) The qualities of the group psychotherapist. In H. I. Kaplan & B. J. Sadock (Eds.), *Comprehensive group psychotherapy* (p. 294) Baltimore: Williams & Wilkins.

James, M. (1981). *Breaking free.* Reading, MA: Addison-Wesley.

James, M. (1977). *Techniques in transactional analysis.* MA: Addison-Wesley.

James, M., & Jongeward, D. (1971). *Born to win.* Reading, MA: Addison-Wesley.

Kahler, T., & Capers, H. (1974). The miniscript. *Transactional Analysis Journal, 4,* 26.

Morrison, J., & O'Hearne, J. (1977). *Practical transactional analysis in management.* Reading, MA: Addison-Wesley.

O'Hearne, J. (1981). Good grief. *Transactional Analysis Journal, 2,* 85.

O'Hearne, J. (1976). How and why do transactional-Gestalt therapists work as they do? *International Journal of Group Psychotherapy, 26,* 163.

Spitz, R. (1945). Hospitalism. *Psychoanalytic Study Child, 1,* 1. 1945.

CHAPTER 17

Psychoanalytic Group Psychotherapy*

J. SCOTT RUTAN

In the practice of psychoanalytic group therapy, tracking unconscious themes, particularly in the transference, is central. In one session, for instance, Susie began the group meeting by saying she had something to say that another member, Karen, a woman she had often experienced as a critical mother, would say is a lie. Susie reported that her biological mother, who gave her up at birth, had reappeared and was demanding to see her, giving no consideration to the effect of this development on Susie. Following a short discussion of this, a second group member, Sandy, tearfully informed the group that her father had just died, leaving her with many bills to pay.

The group empathized with Sandy. Soon Barbara, a third group member, reported a recent encounter with her mother. Coming away, she felt criticized and demeaned. She then observed that she had no positive maternal figures nor girlfriends in her life. She wondered if her difficult relationship with her mother contributed to this void.

The therapist, tracking these verbalizations, understood the group to be struggling with the issues relating to negative parental transference. She heard Barb's observation that "there were no positive maternal figures in her life" as an indication that the transference to the group therapist was also negative. The therapist responded to this comment by saying "I don't count?!! And it seems like no one here feels she will get nurturance from caretakers." Several members nodded, and Barb, smiling, said "I forgot about you."

* Reprinted with permission from Rutan, J. Scott (1993). Psychoanalytic group psychotherapy. In H.I. Kaplan and B.J. Sadock (Eds.) Comprehensive group psychotherapy (3rd ed., pp. 138–146). Lippincott Williams and Wilkins.

INTRODUCTION

Psychoanalytic theory is woven into the fabric of modern society so completely that it is surprising to remember that Sigmund Freud first began work on the theory fewer than 100 years ago. Such analytic principles as the unconscious and transference are largely accepted as givens. Similarly, the use of psychoanalytic principles in group therapy is now commonly accepted.

That was not always the case. Indeed, the psychoanalytic community engaged in heated debate as to the effectiveness of group therapy, in general. Psychopathology was understood to be the result of intrapsychic conflict; thus, treatment consisted of analyzing the individual patient (Freud, 1953–1956). As late as 1958, Lawrence Kubie, an analyst, wrote that group therapy did not offer as powerful a therapeutic modality as did individual therapy (Scheidlinger & Schamess, 1992).

Fundamentally, the questions regarding the efficacious use of psychoanalytic principles in group therapy centered on (1) the possibility of effective transference being generated in the multiperson field of the group and (2) the opportunity for intensive exploration of individual issues in the group setting. Those issues are still not resolved completely, but it is accepted that transference thrives in a group setting, although the nature of the transference is different. Individual patients in group therapy experience peer transferences more quickly and more powerfully than transferences to the authority figure of the leader; those peer transferences become the lens through which inner conflict is examined.

Although it is true that not as much time is available for the intensive exploration of individual histories in the group, it is equally true that the group offers much more opportunity to compare and contrast present perceptions with past experiences. The opportunity to observe patients participating in multiperson interpersonal interactions offers a view on character style that is much richer than that offered in dyadic psychoanalysis. Patients not only speak about their problems but also demonstrate them. In sum, psychoanalytic principles do apply in therapy groups but somewhat differently than in dyadic psychoanalytically oriented psychotherapy and in psychoanalysis proper; indeed, psychoanalytic principles applied in groups offer some unique advantages and healing potential.

HISTORY

Scholars have been intrigued for hundreds of years with the power of groups to alter and affect people. Aristotle, for example, pondered the nature of humans as social animals. Nonetheless, not until the early 1900s did an appreciation of the power of groups become central in the thought of social psychologists. In 1920, both Gustav LeBon and William McDougall examined the curious effects of crowds on the persons who compose them. LeBon, for example, noted: "By the mere fact that he forms part of an organized group, man descends several rungs in the ladder of civilization. Isolated he may be a cultivated individual; in a crowd, he is a barbarian—that is, a creature acting by instinct."

Sigmund Freud was interested in the effect of the group on the individual. His study of group dynamics was a step in his further conceptualization of the superego, and he understood that groups form by adopting the leader as an ego-ideal. As he considered what constitutes a group, in contrast to simply a collection of people, Freud posited that group formation requires having a sense of purpose (goal) and the emergence of clear leadership. Using the theory available to him at the time, he hypothesized that the members develop libidinal ties to the leader. Freud even conducted a group of sorts, his Wednesday evening society. That group, which met in the early 1900s under Freud's leadership, included such luminaries as Alfred Adler, Lou Andreas-Salomé, Hermann Graf, Theodor Reik, Hermann Nunberg, Wilhelm Stekels, Karen Horney, and Fritz Wittles. Stekels originally had the idea for the group as a forum for exchanging ideas and experiences in analyses, but Stekels had also been Freud's patient. Thus, the option of discussing affective and therapeutic issues was built into the group. As documented by the notes of the Vienna Psychoanalytic Society, the meetings became exceedingly passionate at times, finally ending altogether over the conflict between Adler and Freud.

The history of group therapy per se is typically traced to Joseph Pratt, an internist at the Massachusetts General Hospital in Boston. In July 1905, Pratt formed a group of his tuberculosis patients. Pratt's approach was hardly psychoanalytic. Rather, using primarily a lecture format, Pratt relied on an educative approach. Edward Lazell was the first to see psychiatric patients (largely schizophrenic) in groups. However, Lazell's groups at St. Elizabeth's hospital in Washington, D.C., were also primarily lectures and educational in intent.

Trigant Burrow (1928), who treated neurotic patients in groups as early as 1920, was the first to use the phrase "group analysis," although he later exchanged that for the term "phyloanalysis." Burrow, who had met Freud and Sandor Ferenczi and who had studied with Carl Gustav Jung, was an early force in the psychoanalytic movement. Burrow's involvement with group therapy gave a major impetus to the use of psychoanalytic principles in groups.

Others who were in the forefront of invoking psychoanalytic principles in group therapy were Alfred Adler, whose theories about humans being entirely social creatures led naturally to his use of groups as early as 1921; Julius Metzel, who pioneered group work with alcoholic patients in 1927; and Jacob L. Moreno, who founded the school of psychodrama in the 1930s.

Samuel Slavson deserves special recognition because of his instrumental role in the founding of the American Group Psychotherapy Association. Slavson pioneered psychoanalytic group therapy with children in the early 1930s. Throughout his career, he advocated the use of psychoanalytic principles in group therapy (Slavson, 1957). However, Slavson considered group therapy ultimately less powerful and less thorough than individual psychotherapy and psychoanalysis.

Paul Schilder and Louis Wender are often cited as the founders of psychoanalytic group psychotherapy. Schilder (1939), working in the outpatient department of Bellevue Hospital in New York, used psychoanalytic principles in group therapy. Wender was well versed in psychoanalytic theory, having studied with William Alanson White and with Freud himself. He had a powerful influence on Aaron Stein, who later taught hundreds of psychiatric residents at Mt. Sinai Hospital in New York and who, through his emphasis on peer transference, made groupwide interpretations. Furthermore, Wender's writing (1936, 1951) also affected Alexander Wolf and Emanuel Schwartz. Wender was particularly impressed with the ability of groups to recreate the affects from the primary families of the members.

Alexander Wolf and Emanuel Schwartz, who in 1962 wrote *Psychoanalysis in Groups,* can also be cited as the creators of classic psychoanalytic group therapy. Wolf and Schwartz emphasized a focus on the individual in group therapy. Indeed, when Alexander Wolf was cited as a fellow of the American Group Psychotherapy Association, he commented in his remarks, "I have always preferred man to mankind."

Wolf and Schwartz were psychoanalysts, and they adapted their psychoanalytic techniques to the practice of group therapy. Thus, the techniques they emphasized were the classic psychoanalytic techniques of dream interpretation, free association, analysis of resistance, working through, transference, and countertransference. As they wrote, "The function of the group analyst is to guide his patients to fuller awareness and social integration" (Wolf & Schwartz, 1962). That goal is reached through analysis of the transferences that individual members have toward the analyst and other members as displacements. The authors' bias toward focusing on the individual group members as opposed to the group as a whole is evident in such phrases as, "Treating people as if they were identical is sectarian. Differentiating them is humanitarian. Homogeneity sees disagreement as irreconcilable. Heterogeneity sees disagreement as a basis for fruitful exchange." And "Homogenizing influences misunderstand the patient's reactions as collective responses. Personal behavior is discounted except as a manifestation of group influences."

Wolf and Schwartz (1962) continued: "We need, despite our enthusiasm for therapy in a group, to return to psychoanalytic emphasis upon the individual, the individual in interaction. It is not possible to treat a group. We need to keep the patient the center of attention, not an abstraction lost in a sociologic ideal." They remained, however, group therapists: "We are not rejecting groups or group dynamics. We are as interested in groups as the next person..."

Henrietta Glatzer (1965) was perhaps the first to state that classic transference neurosis does appear in group therapy and can be analyzed in that modality. Her focus, like that of Stein and Wolf and Schwartz, was on the individual members of the group.

BASIC PRINCIPLES

Theory

The fundamental principles of psychoanalytic theory remain constant from Freud's earliest hypotheses. Psychoanalytic theory holds that (1) there is psychological determinism, (2) there are unconscious processes, (3) human behavior is dynamic and goal-directed, (4) human development is epigenetic, and (5) functions of the mind are at work at any given point in time (Alonso, 1989; Rutan, 1992).

Psychological Determinism

Psychoanalytic theory is based on the premise that all human behavior and thought are purposeful and lawfully connected. There are no accidents in the psyche. Even the most bizarre behavior is designed to protect the person from pain and can be understood if enough is known about the person.

Unconscious Processes

Perhaps Freud's most radical and useful hypothesis is that an out-of-awareness world, the unconscious, influences perceptions, beliefs, and behaviors. Through the defense mechanism of repression, events, feelings, and traumas that threaten to overwhelm personality are related to that hidden realm. Freud originally understood the unconscious to be determined by the pleasure principle, but he later fixed on an even more primitive force, repetition compulsion, as the driving force in maintaining the unconscious (Freud, 1949). The goal of psychoanalytic therapy is primarily an emotionally and intellectually educative one—to help the patient gain awareness of those parts of the unconscious that lead to destructive present-day misperceptions of the self and the world. Primarily through analysis of slips of the tongue, free association, dreams, and transference, the analyst can assist the patient in gaining insight into the unconscious and mastering the unresolved conflicts that compromise the goals of the adult ego.

Dynamic and Goal-Directed Behavior

All human behavior is goal-directed. Although various schools of psychoanalytic thought posit the goals somewhat differently, they agree that behavior always serves to protect the person from perceived danger or pain. Classic dual-instinct drive theory posits that libido and aggression are innate instincts, with the pleasure principle guiding the psyche toward the reduction of tension. Object relations theory assumes that behavior is innately directed toward gaining relationships and attachments. Self psychology aims to establish and strengthen the integrity of the self.

Epigenetic Development

According to this premise of psychoanalytic theory, personality is formed developmentally. An epigenetic model of development is one in which each stage of development depends on the stage that precedes it. That inevitably places an emphasis on the earliest stages, since they affect all subsequent stages. Psychoanalytic theory is optimistic about human development, in that it assumes that flaws in early stages of development can be repaired if that stage is recalled, relived, and affectively reexperienced correctively in the here and now of the transference.

Functions of the Mind

Psychoanalytic theory assumes that distinct structures of the mind may be in conflict with one another. Freud's classic layers of the mind are the *id* (the primitive instincts and drives), the *superego* (the internalization of culture's and parental expectations), and the *ego* (the monitoring function between the id and the superego). A primary tenet of psychoanalytic theory is that psychological distress occurs subsequent to unconscious conflict between the structures of the mind. The structural model of the mind followed Freud's original topographical model (unconscious, preconscious, conscious). In the topographical model, personality was forged around the charged material contained in the unconscious and the defensive operations maintained to keep that material repressed. In the structural model, psychopathology was viewed not as repressed material intruding into consciousness but, rather, as conflicts between the various structures of the mind.

Technique

Technique always flows from theory. The psychoanalyst faces a fundamental technical problem—an ignorant patient. That is not a pejorative description, since, by definition, all people are ignorant of the unconscious processes. Psychoanalysts attempt to help their patients gain awareness of aspects of themselves of which they not only are unaware but of which they also actively attempt not to become aware, since to do so would result in pain. Thus, the establishment of a good working alliance (Greenson, 1967) is essential. Within the working alliance, there is a hierarchy in the relationship. The therapist works from a position of secondary process, and the patients are asked to relinquish secondary process in favor of primary process. The goal is to help the patients learn the previously unexamined assumptions that guide their perceptions, beliefs, and behaviors—in other words, to make the unconscious conscious.

The art of psychoanalysis is to use the classic windows into the unconscious—free association, slips of the tongue, analysis of the transference, dreams, character style. The multiplicity of relationships in group therapy adds considerable complexity to the task. One of the problems with running therapy groups is that there is a surplus of data. Therapists use theory to sort the data for the most productive use by themselves and their patients.

Roles   Every group therapist is confronted with a variety of choices about what role to assume (Table 1). All the roles have validity from different theoretical perspectives (Kauff, 1979). The psychoanalytic group therapist, however, emphasizes particular points.

Activity-nonactivity   Given the conviction that analyzing transference is a major curative factor, analytic therapists adopt a role that facilitates the emergence of transference. Typically, analytic therapists are more nonactive than active with regard to verbal and physical activity. Ideally, all psychotherapists are active internally—listening, feeling, hypothesizing, empathizing. However,

TABLE I   Roles for the Group Therapist

Activity ⟵——————⟶	Nonactivity
Transparency ⟵——————⟶	Opaqueness
Gratification ⟵——————⟶	Frustration

Table from J. Rutan & W. Stone. (1984). *Psychodynamic group psychotherapy* (p. 118). New York: Macmillan. Used with permission.

psychoanalytic therapists wait for the patient to initiate, rather than setting agendas for the therapy themselves. The waiting results in a meandering, global therapy focused on process rather than content. However, it also results in pervasive therapy designed to reorganize the character traits that result in symptoms, rather than in reducing the symptoms per se.

Transparency–opaqueness   Psychoanalytic group therapists typically do not reveal as much of their own personal lives and reactions as some other therapists do. That is due not to a wish to be withholding (often, it is a difficult role to maintain) but, rather, to a conviction that the best gift one can offer patients is the opportunity to examine their own projections and inner convictions.

Gratification–frustration   Psychoanalytic theory maintains that change occurs most readily as a result of experiencing archaic affects; thus, the therapist does not adopt a gratifying role (which serves to diminish affect). Frustration leads to regression, which allows primitive affects hidden beneath the conscious, maladaptive affects to be experienced. The conscious maladaptive affects are compromise formations and contain unauthentic defensive emotional responses.

Focus   Psychoanalytic theory leads to a number of stereotypical positions in regard to the focus of the therapist's attention.

Past–here and now–future   Psychoanalytic therapy is often misconstrued as a therapy that focuses on the past. In fact, it is very much a here-and-now therapy. Transference, for example, is a here-and-now phenomenon. Nonetheless, it is true that psychoanalytic therapy looks to the past to explain the troublesome distortions in the here and now and seeks to resolve here-and-now problems by resolving archaic unconscious conflicts rooted in the past.

Group as a whole–interpersonal–individuals   One of the hallmarks of psychoanalytic group therapy is its focus on the individuals who make up the group. That does not mean that group-as-a-whole and interpersonal group phenomena are not used in the endeavor. However, psychoanalytic group therapists routinely address individuals and relate their in-group behavior to their individual histories. For psychoanalytic group therapists, groups are vehicles for helping individuals.

In group–out of group   Most psychoanalytic group therapists do not limit group discussions solely to in-group relationships. The group relationships are certainly primary, and there is an assumption that patients will bring their characteristic styles into the group. Nonetheless, the discussion of other relationships (for example, with parents, loved ones, and colleagues) is useful in analyzing the members who make up a group. In all likelihood, the leader's interventions address the here-and-now intragroup transferences.

Affect–cognition   Affect and cognition are both important foci for the analytic therapist. However, affect is the primary focus. Cognition comes after a full expression of affect, when the affect is placed in historical and psychological perspective. Ultimately, useful insight is achieved in the integration of affect and cognition.

Process–content   A primary feature of psychoanalytic theory is a focus on process rather than content. Group process is the corollary of free association in dyadic psychoanalysis. Trusting in the capacity of group process—that is, the unconscious relationships between all group communications and behaviors—the therapist attempts to follow the unconscious thread that weaves its way through each meeting and, indeed, between meetings. Following on the tenet of psychological determinism, psychoanalytic group therapists assume that groups never change the subject. Rather, when it seems that the subject has changed, an unconscious bridge exists between the communications. It is assumed that unconscious communication is evident in the process and, ultimately, is more useful than the content of the verbal material. Analytic therapists look for deep meaning beneath content communications.

Understanding–corrective emotional experience   All psychotherapy includes elements of corrective emotional experience. The opportunity to be in a group where one feels accepted, heard, and valued is, in itself, corrective. Nonetheless, psychoanalytic therapy does not assume that corrective emotional experience is the most powerful change agent. Rather, understanding (insight) is assumed to result in the most powerful and enduring change.

TABLE II   Foci for the Group Therapist

Past ⟵——————— (Here and now) ———————⟶ Future
Group as a whole ⟵——— (Interpersonal) ———⟶ Individuals
In group ⟵————————————————⟶ Out of group
Affect ⟵————————————————⟶ Cognition
Process ⟵————————————————⟶ Content
Understanding ⟵———⟶ Corrective emotional experience

Table from J. Rutan & W. Stone. (1984). *Psychodynamic group psychotherapy* (p. 118). New York: Macmillan. Used with permission.

Case Example   The following snapshot in the movie of a group is not an intensive exploration of group therapy but, rather, a heuristic exercise designed to tease out the salient factors for review.

A psychoanalytic group had been meeting for several years. The group members were hardworking and dedicated to the process. The members routinely associated freely during the sessions, brought dreams for analysis, and confronted one another.

Sam was a successful businessman. His father committed suicide when he was 10, and Sam took on the role of man of the house. He reported that his mother was loving, if longsuffering, and he felt that his mother loved him (the oldest) more than her other two sons. Sam had been struggling with his 10-year-old son; he reported that the son was challenging and rebellious, both at home and at school.

Susan was a mental health professional who struggled with depression. Her father was a physician, and her mother was an angry woman who felt that she had sacrificed her career as a singer to be a wife and mother. Susan confronted Sam: "You are probably teaching your son to be rebellious. How else can he get your attention? You are always involved in your business. Business, not family, is your first love."

Sam fired back: "Don't confuse me with your father. He was busy healing the world and forgot to take care of you. When you have that tone in your voice, you must sound like your mother."

John, known as the group peacemaker, intervened quickly: "I think Susan was trying to help, Sam." Susan corrected him: "No, I was telling him he was a lousy father and he'd better give more attention to his son while there is still time."

At that point, Judy interrupted: "Did I mention that I may be getting a job out of state? I may have to leave the group."

The therapist could respond to that impassioned moment in the group in a variety of ways. Even within the psychoanalytic tradition, the exchange could be viewed from almost any point on any of the axes. However, stereotypical places on the axes define the psychoanalytic position.

For example, with regard to the roles the leader might adopt, the psychoanalytic group therapist typically adopts a nonactive stance. In the vignette, the therapist's activity would be inward, observing, hypothesizing, listening for unconscious material, attending to his or her affects. The leader would not actively intervene to interrupt, facilitate, or defuse the interactions but, rather, would observe them as they unfolded.

The psychoanalytic role of opaqueness results in the therapist's not introducing reactions to the interactions. The therapist might well believe that one or another patient is right in a particular confrontation with another but would not make that opinion public. Rather, the therapist remains neutral and allows the patients to place attributes (through transference) onto and into the therapist.

The analytic therapist does not gratify, meaning that the goal is not to reduce anxiety and tension. The therapist would not move to reduce the heat of the exchange. Rather, the therapist would allow as much affect as possible, to observe the participants' defenses and character styles.

In terms of where psychoanalytic group therapists focus attention, likely, they would begin with the here and now, elaborating the affects experienced in the exchange. The goal of the endeavor, however, would be to deduce from those here-and-now affects the conflicted issues from the past that contaminate the present. Sam, it might be hypothesized, was having particular trouble with his son at that time because the son was the same age as Sam was when Sam's father died. It may be that Sam was reexperiencing some powerful affects from his own youth as he observed his son. Indeed, some of the rebelliousness in the son, as Susan suggested, may be the unacceptable rebelliousness that Sam himself wanted to exhibit as a child and that he now projected onto his son. Likewise, Susan's immediate and powerful angry reaction to Sam and her understanding that the root of the problem was Sam's involvement in his business may well have been a present-day reliving of her rage at her father. As Sam so unempathically pointed out, her father did spend time caring for others more than for his family.

It is assumed that all the behaviors of all the members are rooted in character and, therefore, history. John, for example, was the peacemaker in his own alcoholic family. He routinely tried to diminish affect in the group, since, in his history, the stirring of affect inevitably culminated in physical violence.

The focus of the leader begins with the interpersonal, examining and elaborating the affects in the group relationships. The data gleaned from those exchanges is then used to provide information to the individuals regarding the connections between present behaviors, thoughts, and feelings and the past. Thus, the leader would probably have as a goal for John that he understand his present dread of affect as related to the place of affect in his family of origin. That would help him to allow appropriate affect in his here-and-now relationships.

Psychoanalytic group therapists value out-of-group material. That is not to imply that members are encouraged to have out-of-group relationships with one another. Quite the contrary; most psychoanalytic group therapists maintain that the group can function most productively if the members restrict their relationships to the group. Out-of-group material is information that comes from elsewhere than the group interactions themselves. The most obvious examples in the vignette above were the references to Sam's son, Sam's father, and Sue's father. Nonetheless, the psychoanalytic group therapist typically begins by a full exploration of the in-group interactions. Indeed, the expectation is that the important distortions in the members' relationships eventually occur in the in-group relationships. The psychoanalytic position, however, is that it is insufficient to analyze only the in-group relationships. Rather, it is hoped that those relationships can be used to understand the out-of-group relationships, such as those with family, loved ones, and work colleagues.

Affect is the primary data of psychoanalytic psychotherapy. However, affect is insufficient to provide insight and change. Catharsis, although useful, does not result in change, according to psychoanalytic theory. Rather, affect is used as a vehicle in understanding the underlying conflict. Cognition is important in providing linkage between the present affect and past learning. In the vignette, most psychoanalytic group therapists would encourage the expression of affect between Sam, Sue, and John before attempting to understand the interactions and to provide cognitive closure.

The psychoanalytic therapist always tries to listen to process rather than simply content. Thus, although it felt as though Judy had changed the subject and disregarded the charged exchange between Sam, Susan, and John, it is assumed that there must have been a connection. The psychoanalytic question is, "Why did Judy choose that particular moment to speak?" Judy's mother was a volatile person who would, when offended, storm out of the house and disappear for days. One day, she disappeared forever. In the light of her history, Judy's behavior could be viewed as an identification with her mother—a temptation to flee the group, rather than bear the affect.

Many forms of psychotherapy rely primarily on a corrective emotional experience model of change. That is, the therapeutic situation offers patients a different and healthier response than what they expect from history. Psychoanalytic theory, although it incorporates aspects of that school, relies on understanding as the primary curative factor. Thus, the therapist would help the participants in the vignette understand the influence of history and life experience on their present exchange to free them from the distortions they brought to the current situation.

Applications

Dyadic psychoanalysis has limited applicability. It is along, intense, costly endeavor that requires ego strength, intelligence, motivation, and financial resources on the part of the patient. Furthermore, the patient is restricted to the analyst's limited responses. Psychoanalytic group therapy has much broader applicability, since the members of the group have the holding environment of the group, along with the sustaining relationships offered there, to assist with the arduous process of therapy. Furthermore, in group therapy, the other members can often assist individual members in overcoming resistance, observing repetitive patterns, and gaining insight into their transferences in ways that therapists cannot. Colleagues in therapy groups, not limited by the therapist's role, can offer honest and spontaneous feedback to one another. Attempting insight-oriented, character-changing psychotherapy with seriously ill patients is time-consuming, but the principles work with almost any patients who can commit to the task. Primitive patients seem to be able to make better use of classic psychoanalytic techniques in group settings than in dyadic therapy.

Strengths and Weaknesses

The strengths and the weaknesses of psychoanalytic theory correlate nicely. That is, the expansiveness of the theory and the therapy goals lend themselves to long, intensive psychotherapies designed to bring about character change beyond symptom relief. The time required does not always meet with the patient's expectations or even the patient's needs. Furthermore, the ego strength and the cognitive ability required to engage in a treatment that focuses on transferences and unconscious conflicts mean that certain patients make exceedingly slow use of the modality. Nonetheless, if the goal is to bring about fundamental character change, no theory or set of techniques has yet appeared that holds as much promise as psychodynamic psychotherapy.

New Directions

Psychoanalytic theory is incredibly vital. Modifications to Freud's classic instinct theory are being made from several sources. Self psychology and the followers of Heinz Kohut (1971, 1977) have added the concept of self as a primary factor in the emergence of personality. The British object relations school, originating with Klein (1946), maintains that the drive to attachment is primary. Ego psychology (A. Freud, 1954) stresses the importance of defenses. Feminist theory seeks an integration of psychoanalytic theory, the study of gender, and development (Chodorow, 1989). These are only a few of the important schools of modern psychoanalytic thought. The common theme in all these modifications of classic Freudian theory is an emphasis on the interpersonal factors involved in personality and pathology and the effects of interpersonal factors on cure.

The modern stress on the interpersonal fits nicely with the use of psychoanalytic principles in group therapy. For example, clinicians now realize that transference occurs not only vertically (for example, to authority and parental figures) but also horizontally (to peers). Those peer transferences are uniquely available to the group therapist for analysis.

The concept of countertransference and the role of the therapist's persona are continually being reviewed and revised in modern psychoanalytic theory. Whereas countertransference was originally understood as an unconscious pathological distortion by the therapist because of unresolved conflicts, that concept is being broadened to include the therapist's entire conscious and unconscious affective response to the interpersonal field of the patient–therapist interaction. Through such mechanisms as projective identification, the therapist's affect is often induced by the character style of the patient and is a source of powerful diagnostic data. The mutual contributions of the therapist and the patient to the affective responses of each other represent a major point of ongoing discussion and thought among psychoanalytic theorists. As Gill (1982) stated, "uncontaminated transference" cannot exist. The result of the ongoing investigation is that psychoanalytic therapists are no longer as opaque as they once were. The stereotype of the psychoanalyst as "cadaver" (Stone, 1961) no longer applies. Therapists are beginning to understand that a more human therapist does not diminish the power of transference in the therapy. In the highly personal and human interactions of group therapy, therapists must not conceive of themselves as impersonal in role.

It is a truism that psychoanalytic psychotherapy is under siege in this age of managed care. The duration of treatment required by the method and the difficulty in assigning specific goals for specific time frames of treatment mean that many managed-care systems do not reimburse adequately for psychoanalytically oriented treatment. Psychoanalytic therapists must come down from the lofty position of unchallenged experts and devise valid research methods that will document the effectiveness of the modality.

Research Findings

Psychoanalytic theory does not lend itself easily to empirical research. How does one measure happiness, anxiety, depression? Researchers have tried for decades to find trustworthy empirical measures to use in the endeavor. In recent years, the work of Luborsky (1984), Hartley and Strupp (1983), and others have made major progress in bringing a solid research foundation to the work of psychoanalytic psychotherapists.

Psychanalytic group therapy has also been the subject of much research in recent years (Burnand, 1990; Dies, 1990; Tillitski, 1990). Those studies are documenting the effectiveness of psychodynamic group psychotherapy as an effective therapeutic modality.

As qualitative research gains increasing respect in science, the exploration of group processes and their effects on health and pathology also finds more robust support.

REFERENCES

Alonso, A. (1989). The psychodynamic approach. In A. Lazare (Ed.), *Psychiatry: Diagnosis and treatment* (2nd ed., p. 37). Baltimore: Williams & Wilkins.

Brigham, P. M. (1992). Object relations and regression in groups. *International Journal of Group Psychotherapy, 42,* 247.

Burnand, G. (1990). Group development phases as working through six fundamental human problems. *Small Group Research, 2,* 255.

Burrow, T. (1928). The basis of group-analysis, or the analysis of the reactions of normal and neurotic individuals. *British Journal of Medical Psychology, 8,* 198.

Chodorow, N. (1989). *Feminism and psychoanalytic theory.* New Haven: Yale Univ. Press,

Dies, R. (1990). Clinician and researcher: Mutual growth through dialogue. In S. Tuttman (Ed.), *Expanding domains of psychodynamic group therapy* (p. 213). Madison, CT: International Universities Press.

Durkin, H. E. (1964). *The group in depth.* New York: International Universities Press.

Freud, A. (1954). Psychoanalysis and education. *Psychoanalytic Study of the Child, 9,* 5.

Freud, S. (1953–1966). The dynamics of transference. In *Standard edition of the complete psychological works of Sigmund Freud* (Vol. 12, p. 99). London: Hogarth Press.

Freud, S. (1953–1966.) The ego and the id. In *Standard edition of the complete psychological works of Sigmund Freud* (Vol. 19, p. 57). London, UK: Hogarth Press.

Freud, S. (1953–1966). Five lectures on psychoanalysis. In *Standard edition of the complete psychological works of Sigmund Freud* (Vol. 11, p. 3). London, UK: Hogarth Press.

Freud, S. (1953–1966). Fragment of an analysis of a case of hysteria. In *Standard edition of the complete psychological works of Sigmund Freud* (Vol. 7, p. 3). London, UK: Hogarth Press.

Freud, S. (1953–1966). The two classes of instincts. In *Standard edition of the complete psychological works of Sigmund Freud* (Vol. 19, p. 40). London, UK: Hogarth Press.

Gill, M. M. (1982). *Analysis of transference.* New York: International Universities Press.

Glatzer, H. (1965). Aspects of transference in group psychotherapy. *International Journal of Group Psychotherapy, 15,* 167.

Greenson, R. (1967). *The technique ad practice of psychoanalysis.* New York: International Universities Press.

Hartley, D., & Strupp, H. (1983). The therapeutic alliance: Its relationship to outcome in brief psychotherapy. *Empirical Studies in Psychoanalytic Theories, 1,* 1.

Kauff, P. (1993). The contribution of analytic group therapy to the psychoanalytic process. In A. Alonso & H. Swiller (Eds.), *Group therapy in clinical practice* (p. 136). Washington: American Psychiatric Press.

Kauff, P. (1979). Diversity in analytic group psychotherapy. *International Journal of Group Psychotherapy, 29,* 51.

Klein, M. (1946). Notes on some schizoid mechanisms. *International Journal of Psychoanalysis, 27,* 99.

Kohut, H. (1971). *The analysis of the self.* New York: International Universities Press.

Kohut, H. (1977). *The restoration of the self.* New York: International Universities Press.

Lazell, E. (1921). The group treatment of dementia praecox. *Psychoanalytic Review, 8,* 168.

LeBon, G. (1920). *The crowd: A study of the popular mind.* New York: Fisher, Unwin.

Luborsky, L. (1984). *Principles of psychoanalytic psychotherapy.* New York: Basic Books.

McDougall, W. (1907). *The group mind.* New York: Putnam's.

Pratt, J. (1907). The class method of treating consumption in the homes of the poor. *JAMA, 49,* 755.

Rutan, J. (1992). Psychodynamic group psychotherapy. *International Journal of Group Psychotherapy, 42,* 19.

Rutan, J., & Stone, W. (1984). *Psychodynamic group psychotherapy.* New York: Macmillan.

Scheidlinger, S., & Schamess, G. (1992). 50 years of AGPA 1942–1992: An overview. In K. R. MacKenzie (Ed.), *Classics in group psychotherapy* (Vol. 1). New York: Guilford.

Schilder, P. (1939). Results and problems in group psychotherapy in severe neuroses. *Mental Hygiene, 23,* 87.

Slavson, S. (1957). Are there "group dynamics" in therapy groups? *International Journal of Group Psychotherapy, 7,* 131.

Stolorow, R. D. (1992). Closing the gap between theory and practice with better psychoanalytic theory. *Psychotherapy: Theory, Research, and Practice, 29,* 159.

Stone, L. (1961). *The psychoanalytic situation.* New York: International Universities Press.

Strupp, H. H. (1992). The future of psychodynamic psychotherapy. *Psychotherapy: Theory, Research, and Practice, 29,* 21.

Tillitski, C. (1990). A meta-analysis of estimated effect sizes for group versus individual versus control treatments. *International Journal of Group Psychotherapy, 40,* 215.

Wender, L. (1951). Current trends in group psychotherapy. *American Journal of Psychotherapy, 5,* 381.

Wender, L. (1936). The dynamics of group psychotherapy and its application. *Journal of Nervous and Mental Disorders, 84,* 54.

Wolf, A., & Schwartz, E. K. (1962). *Psychoanalysis in groups.* New York: Grune & Stratton.

CHAPTER 18

Termination

JOHN R. PRICE AND DAVID R. HESCHELES

Lucille was referred by a colleague who was supervising her medication following a suicide attempt. Two of Lucille's brothers had committed suicide, and Lucille had made previous attempts.

She had, in recent years, divorced her husband of 26 years. All her married life, she had given to and done for her husband and four, now adult, offspring. So, emotionally exhausted, she joined a therapy group.

In the course of 14 months in group, she learned to ask for herself, to define and hold to boundaries when it came to her family's inroads on her, and both to receive nurturance from her fellow group members and to nurture herself.

COGNITIVE BEHAVIORAL FOCAL GROUPS

Termination in Focal groups is tied to the time and duration which has been clearly specified within the initial orientation. Often, focal groups will try to negotiate additional sessions with the leader, as though there will be tremendous additional progress made. This is usually not the case and needs to be avoided. The request for more time is usually based on fear of relapse and the painful recognition of an important, worthwhile experience ending. These concerns need to be addressed directly.

The termination in Focal groups, similar to that in short-term, psychodynamic groups, is utilized to focus the therapy and expedite the therapeutic work. Tying everything together is a typical issue dealt with during the termination stage of Focal groups.

LONG-TERM PSYCHODYNAMIC GROUPS AND ECLECTIC GROUPS

Although a client's termination from a group is hardly a part of starting groups, it is, nonetheless, something about which you want to do some thinking before you enter the arena. Earlier, you gave your clients a copy of your ground rules for group. Number five of the ground rules asks a client not to make a sudden, unilateral decision about leaving the group. Rather, in the ground rules, the client was asked to spend some sessions talking about the desire to graduate.

A successful graduation goes something like this: A client will bring up *in* the group the possibility of graduating. After some discussion, he or she gets agreement from group members and the therapist that, yes, graduation seems imminent and appropriate. The client completes his or her work in another few sessions and bids the group goodbye.

Frequently, however, when a group member mentions graduating or leaving the group, other group members or the therapist question the client's decision. The client will often rethink the decision after the group has discussed the pending departure. She or he may clarify the reasons for entering the group in the first place and then postpone the graduation until a later and more appropriate time.

For instance, one client had gotten past the emotional crisis regarding the decision to divorce and mistook the sense of relief for a readiness to graduate from group therapy. His original goal was not just to make a decision about staying married but also to work on some more basic characterological issues. He stayed with the group until he met his more fundamental goals.

Another client had gotten past her attempts to parent her 45-year-old son. However, she still had not dealt with her interference with other family members. The therapist and the group helped her see that she had not yet met her wider goals. She stayed until she had done so.

Had the aforementioned clients not reconsidered their decisions after input from the group and the therapist, they would have terminated unsuccessfully. That is, they would have mistaken the immediate relief they felt for a more inclusive readiness to graduate.

While clients do not need the permission of the therapist or the group members to leave the group, they are encouraged to take those observations and suggestions into account while deciding about termination. The unsuccessful terminee may be one who has not used group appropriately all along. She or he may not have attended to input from members of the group, and the premature decision to terminate may be yet another unilateral action.

Clients who, for whatever reason, do not run the course provide the therapist with an opportunity to retrospectively evaluate the decision to put them into a psychotherapy group. For example, the therapist may realize that a given client's narcissism was too fixed to permit that client to become integrated into the group.

There are those clients who seemingly understand the nature of a psychotherapy group, its purpose and goals, but who turn out to have only paid lip service to the process. Again, you as the therapist have the opportunity to reevaluate the appropriateness of your original decision to put that particular client into a therapy group.

SHORT-TERM PSYCHODYNAMIC GROUPS

The above discussion of termination applies to long-term psychodynamic groups. In short-term psychodynamic groups in which there are fluid, easy entrance and exit policies, the work is conceptualized as a stage of therapy being completed. The group member has set specific goals to be completed in a specific time frame. The group member does not think she or he has graduated but has finished a piece of work or negotiated a state of life. The group member leaves, entertaining the notion that she may be back in therapy in the future to complete other pieces of therapeutic work which are impairing her life's functioning. In short-term groups, termination is utilized more as a way of focusing the treatment and expediting the therapeutic work.

CHAPTER 19

Your Role as Therapist

JOHN R. PRICE AND DAVID R. HESCHELES

Sam, an enthusiastic postgraduate trainee in group psychotherapy, reported in his supervisory section meeting that he was beginning to get uncomfortable comments from colleagues with whom he socialized. Careful listening on the part of his supervisor allowed her to gently point out to him that a dinner party was not a therapy group.

Basic to the successful group is your role. In the least complicated of your roles, you, as leader, are the technical expert. You make interpretations at the appropriate moment. In the event the group gets stuck in any given session, it is your decision about when, how, and *whether* to intervene to help.

Many of these decisions will be determined by your theoretical orientation. The Psychodynamic group therapist will choose one path, while the Eclectic therapist may choose another. This issue is not which is the more correct path but, rather, whether the therapist is operating consistently within her or his theoretical framework.

Another important role for the therapist is modeling. As the therapist, you offer a model of nonjudgmental acceptance regarding whatever substantive material a group member brings up in group. You show trust in the group member and the group process when someone discloses information that might make that member feel vulnerable.

From David: It is my hope that this book will encourage psychotherapists to start groups. For me, the groups I lead are the most exciting, challenging, gratifying aspect of my professional week. They often are a powerful, moving experience.

It is often difficult for the therapist to get his or her groups started—many times due to fears of exposure, attack, and loss of control. Once these anxieties are resolved, you, as a therapist, will add to your therapeutic toolkit a powerful, effective intervention that will be exciting and growth-producing, as well as help you survive in the current economic environment.

From John: If we have accomplished our goal in writing this *Guide,* you, the reader, should be more comfortable about the prospect of starting a psychotherapy group. To repeat, the goal was not to teach the reader how to run a group, although some of these issues have been addressed here; rather, it was to systematically address various issues and strategies in getting a group started.

Prior to the current preeminence of managed-care organizations and the attendant difficulty in referral flow, I maintained ten psychotherapy groups in a private practice setting. The approaches in this guide were used in accomplishing this.

Maintain your optimism. I wish you the best!

Helpful Names and Addresses

The American Group Psychotherapy Association (AGPA), 25 East 21st Street, 6th Floor, New York, NY 10010. Phone: 212-477-2677; Fax: 212-979-6627.

The American Psychological Association, Division 49, Group Psychology and Group Psychotherapy, 750 First Street NE, Washington, DC 20002. Phone: 202-336-5500; Fax: (Division Services) 202-218-3599.

The Fielding Institute, 2112 Santa Barbara Street, Santa Barbara, CA 93105. Phone: 806-687-9793; Fax: 805-687-9793; http://www.fielding.edu.

National Registry of Certified Group Psychotherapists (NRCGP), 25 East 21st Street, 6th Floor, New York, NY 10010. Phone: 212-477-1600.

Psychotherapy Finances P. O. Box 8979, Jupiter, FL 33468-8979. Phone: 561-624-1155; Fax: 561-624-6006.

Introduction to Group Psychotherapy

JOHN R. PRICE

Progress in therapy, I've learned from experience, is most readily obtained in a group rather than in individual, one-on-one sessions. Because we live in groups—families, neighborhoods, fellow workers, fellow students, fellow parishioners—it is both easier to identify an individual's dysfunction within a group setting and easier to treat the individual within a group. How often do you or I see a physician, a dentist, a lawyer, a clergyman by ourselves, alone, in a year's time? Not nearly as often as we are in a group working, playing, socializing.

I'd like to spend a few minutes with you describing how I do group psychotherapy, going over three areas with you: (1) the ground rules for the conduct of a group, (2) some administrative details, and (3) my style as a therapist.

The ground rules for group meetings provide emotional safety for the group. The rules help define a safe place in which people can come to practice new behaviors, to change their emotional reactions to things, and to give up various dysfunctional behaviors. There are five ground rules.

The *first* ground rule has to do with CONFIDENTIALITY. Each member entering a group agrees not to reveal the identity of any other member of the group to anybody outside of the group, either by name or other identifying information. You wouldn't feel comfortable in talking about yourself if you thought you were going to be talked about. You *are* free, however, to talk to a friend or family member about your *own* work in the group, but you are *not* free to talk about the work that others do. Doing so might reveal the identity of that other person.

Second, there is no ground rule prohibiting CONTACT between members between group sessions. However, if there is contact, you must feel that you could SHARE it with the group. For example, you're a member of a group and, one day, after the group meets, another member says in the hall, "Let's have lunch together this week, but I'd rather the group not know about it." That's contrary to the rules. If, however, neither of you cares if the group knows that you had lunch together, then go have lunch and enjoy yourselves.

The *third* ground rule: NO SEX between members of the group as long as you are members of the group. Growth and change can occur through caring and sharing. For example, Sarah says to Sam, "I think you're a beautiful human being." Receiving such a loving stroke, Sam can come to feel better about himself. Sarah can grow by sharing some of her caring feelings. Applying the no-sex rule, Sarah is not making herself vulnerable sexually, nor is Sam under any pressure to make sexual overtures to Sarah. Both individuals are protected, and so is the group. However, were two members of the group to start having a sexual relationship, it would create a powerful emotional undercurrent between two individuals that would damage the integrity of the group as a working unit.

The *fourth* ground rule: NO VIOLENCE. This means no hitting each other or tearing up the office. Growth and change can occur through anger *verbally* expressed. Some time ago in one of my groups, a man began talking about his wife in an abusive way. The woman sitting next to him recognized that he was treating his wife in the same way she was being treated by her husband. The woman got furious with him. In the next 5 minutes, he learned more from her about himself and how he was treating *his* wife than he could have learned from anyone else in the group, myself included. She learned about the depths of her hostility toward her husband who, as it turned out, was about to divorce her. Both people profited from the confrontation, and the group learned a tremendous amount the constructive use of anger.

Fifth, and finally, I ask you, as you go into group psychotherapy, to agree that when the time comes that you think about leaving the group, you DIS-CUSS this with the group rather than tell me by telephone or leave a message with my secretary that you are not returning to the group. I ask that you not wait until your last session to bring up the subject of leaving. Instead, allow yourself and the group a few sessions to discuss your decision to leave. Since your relationship with the group members is involved, it's important to dis-cuss this in group rather than with me individually. One reason for this is that, occasionally, clients will feel uncomfortable in the group and start thinking about leaving just as they are about to turn a corner in their ther-apy, but they are unaware of that corner ahead of them. Having agreed to this ground rule, they will discuss their discomfort and their desire to leave. By doing so, they can be helped to see what they are running from. Then, they can make a decision about whether and when they want to work on this scary situation. Another reason for discussing your departure is that mem-bers need to know whether they can count on you for help and support. We must not abandon one another.

Again, these ground rules protect individual members and preserve the integrity of the group as a working unit.

Next, I'd like to talk about some administrative details of group. The group meets in my office once a week for 90 minutes. The maximum size of a group is eight members. The fees are on a monthly basis. In those months during which there are five sessions, the fifth is free. You are not billed for it. By the same token, if you miss a session, you still pay for it. Each person is being charged for a place in the group that is being reserved for him, to do with as he sees fit, including the decision as to whether to attend or not. Unless clients are filing their own insurance claims, our office files the claim each month for the sessions attended. Clients are responsible for payment of the sessions not attended.

The third and final area I'd like to address has to do with my style as a group therapist. I believe in keeping group as much like the real world as possible. I keep a balance between males and females in my groups. Males and females are divided about half and half in the world we live in. I assign individuals to a group on the basis of places available rather than by the individuals' problems. If you polled your neighborhood, you'd find the full range of problems represented, just as you would in a therapy group. Furthermore, you'd find a range of ages in your neighborhood, as you would in a group. However, I don't work with adolescents or children.

Finally, it is your responsibility in a group to decide *what* you want to work on and *when*. It is my responsibility to provide the *how to* expertise after you have identified what you want to work on. Therefore, I do not *call* on people in the group. If Sam, for instance, has worked for about 20 minutes and then says, "I feel good about this—I'd like to stop here," I might respond, "Good piece of work, Sam." Then you might see me gazing out the window, looking at the carpet or my desktop. The point is that, if I started scanning the room after Sam finished his work and I settled my gaze on Louise, it might seem I was saying, "Well, Louise, it's your turn to go to work." Now, I have no idea what's going on in Louise's head after she's heard Sam do his work. Therefore, I avoid even *eye* contact so as not to inadvertently call on someone. Let's say that Suzie speaks up after Sam has finished and says she has some work she wants to do. I will reply, "Okay, Suzie, you're on."

I apply to new members this same principle of each determining his or her own pace. Let's say it's your first time in group and you're out in the waiting room with a bunch of chatting people. At the appointed time, I'll come out and bring everybody into the office. In a few seconds, when the chatting stops, I'll turn to you and say, "Well, John, would you like to introduce yourself?" You'll say, "I'm John Doe," and the next person will say, "I'm Esther Reinecke," "Dorothy Runyan," "Ted Schwartz," "Bob Moore," and so forth. When the circle is complete and it's back to you, I'll say, "Make it easy on yourself, John, on getting into why you are here. If you want to jump right in and talk about why you and I thought group therapy would be good for you, feel free to do so. If, on the other hand, you wish to be an observer and get to know these folks as you see how a group works, you're free to do that." Then, if you're like about 98% of all new members in group, you will probably say, "I think I'll listen for a while," at which point I will break contact with you. Every group member has, at one time or another, been the new member and can understand the apprehension you may feel. Therefore, no one will press you to talk about yourself until you're ready to speak up.

This, in a rather large nutshell, is how I do groups. Give it some thought and, in the next session or so, we'll talk about your reaction and your decision. I'm giving you this summary so that you don't have to concern yourself about remembering details. Please read it over. I believe it will help you understand how groups work and why group psychotherapy is successful.

A Consumer's Guide to Group Psychotherapy*

ABOUT GROUP PSYCHOTHERAPY

Group psychotherapy is a special form of therapy in which a small number of people meet together under the guidance of a professionally trained therapist to help themselves or one another. The therapy has been widely used and has been a standard treatment option for over 50 years.

If you stop and think about it, each of us has been raised in group environment, either through our families, schools, organized activities, or work. These are the environments, in which we grow and develop as human beings. Group psychotherapy is no different. It provides a place where you come together with others to share problems or concerns, to better understand your own situation, and to learn from and with each other.

Group therapy helps people improve their interpersonal relationships. It addresses feelings of isolation, depression or anxiety. And it helps people make significant changes so they feel better about the quality of their lives.

Group works! In studies comparing group psychotherapy to individual therapy, group therapy has been shown to be as effective and sometimes even more effective. In cases of medical illness, there is substantial evidence that this form of therapy helps people cope better with their illness, enhances the quality of their lives and, in some cases, such as breast cancer, has even been shown to help people live longer.

If you are considering therapy, together you and your therapist can explore the nature of your problem. You will work to develop a better understanding of the problem and discuss what changes might make the situation better. In addition to group therapy, there are several other options available, including:

* Reprinted with permission from the American Group Psychotherapy Association, Inc.

- Talking with an individual therapist
- Participating in therapy as a couple or family
- Receiving medication
- A combination of the above treatments

Your therapist can help you understand the benefits of each of these treatment options and determine what's right for you.

THE GROUP PSYCHOTHERAPIST

Group psychotherapists are mental health professionals trained in one of several areas: psychiatry, psychology, social work, psychiatric nursing, marriage and family therapy, pastoral counseling, creative arts counseling or substance abuse counseling. In considering a therapist for group, make sure he or she has had a level of training that meets your particular needs and is also qualified to lead group psychotherapy. The National Registry of Certified Group Psychotherapists certifies group therapists by the designation "CGP," which means the therapist has received specialized training and is experienced in group therapy. Clinical Members of the American Group Psychotherapy Association (AGPA) also have received specialized training.

WHO CAN BENEFIT

Like individual therapy, group therapy can benefit almost anyone. Some of the issues typically addressed include:

- Difficulties with interpersonal relationships
- Problems in children and adolescents (such as the impact of a divorce, peer issues, learning or behavioral problems)
- Aging
- Medical illness
- Dealing with loss
- Gay, Lesbian and bisexual adults
- Personality disorders
- Addictive disorders

THE GROUP THERAPY SESSION

The group therapy session is a collaborative effort in which the therapist assumes clinical responsibility for the group and its members. In a typical session, which lasts about 75-90 minutes, members work to express their own problems, feelings, ideas and reactions as freely and honestly as possible. Such exploration gives the group the important information needed to understand and help one another. Members learn not only to understand themselves and their own issues but also become "therapeutic helpers" for other members.

COMMONLY ASKED QUESTIONS

How Does Group Work?

A group therapist appropriately selects people (usually 5 to 10) who would be helped by the group experience and who can be learning partners for one another. In meetings, people are encouraged to talk with each other in a spontaneous and honest fashion. A professionally trained therapist, who provides productive examination of the issues or concerns affecting the individuals and the group, guides the discussion.

Not every group is alike. There are a variety of styles that different groups use. For instance , some focus more on interpersonal development, where much of the learning actually comes from the interaction of members themselves. Others address cognitive behaviors, where the emphasis is on learning how to control negative thoughts, address phobias or relieve anxiety-inducing situations.

If Someone Is in a Group, Do They Also Need Individual Therapy?

It depends on the individual. Sometimes group therapy is used as the main or only treatment approach. Sometimes it's used along with individual therapy. Often people find that working simultaneously in both group and individual therapy stimulates growth in mutually complementary ways. And clients may see two different therapists for individual and group therapies. In such cases, it's generally considered important for the two therapists to communicate with each other periodically for the client's benefit. Ask your therapist about the type of therapy that will best meet your needs.

How Is Group Therapy Different from Support Groups and Self-Help Groups?

Group therapy focuses on interpersonal relationships and helps individuals learn how to get along better with other people under the guidance of a professional coach. Group psychotherapy also provides a support network of specific problems or challenges. The psychotherapy group is different from self-help and support groups in that it not only helps people cope with their problems, but also provides for change and growth. Self-help groups usually focus on a particular shared symptom or situation and are usually not led by a trained therapist. Support groups, which are generally led by professionals, help people cope with difficult situations at various times but are not geared toward change.

WHY IS GROUP THERAPY USEFUL?

When someone is thinking about joining a group, it's normal for them to have questions or concerns. What am I going to get out of this? Will there be enough time to deal with my own problems in a group setting? What if I don't like the people in my group?

Joining a group is useful because it provides opportunities to learn with and from other people, to understand one's own patterns of thought and behavior and those of others, and to perceive how group members react to one another. We live and interact with people every day and often there are things that other people are experiencing or grappling with that can be beneficial to share with others. In group therapy, you learn that perhaps you're not as different as you think or that you're not alone. You'll meet and interact with people, and the whole group learns to work on shared problems-one of the most beneficial aspects. The more you involve yourself in the group, the more you get out of it.

WHAT KINDS OF PEOPLE SHOULD PARTICIPATE IN GROUP THERAPY?

Group therapy can benefit many different people, from those having difficulties with interpersonal relationships to those dealing with specific problems such as a serious medical illness, loss, addictive disorders or behavioral problems. With adolescents, for example, group therapy teaches socialization skills needed to help function in environments outside the home.

WILL THERE BE PEOPLE WITH SIMILAR PROBLEMS IN MY GROUP?

The therapist's role is to evaluate each member's problems prior to forming the group. Usually there is a mix of members who can learn from each other.

While some members will have similar circumstances, it's not necessary for all members in the group to be dealing with exactly the same problem.

What Kind of Commitment Do I Need to Make?

The time commitment depends on the type of group and the nature and extent of your problems. Short-term groups devoted to concrete issues can last anywhere from 6 to 20 weeks. Support therapy groups (for example, those dealing with a medical illness such as cancer) may be more long-term. There are also more open-ended groups in which members work at their own pace and leave when their particular needs or goals have been met. It's best to talk with your therapist to determine the length of time that's right for you.

What if I'm Uncomfortable Discussing My Problems in Front of Others?

It's not unusual to feel uneasy or embarrassed when first joining a group, but soon you begin to develop feelings of interest and trust. Most clients find that group therapy provides a great deal of relief because it allows them a chance to talk with others who are experiencing similar problems-in a private, confidential setting, Many people who have experienced group therapy believe that working together with others is helpful and they feel better by participating in this form of therapy.

What Does Group Cost?

The cost varies depending on the type of therapist and perhaps even the geographic area of the country. Typically, group therapy is about half the price of individual therapy.

Is It Covered by Insurance?

Insurance coverage is similar for both group and individual therapy. In addition, most managed care companies cover group much the same as individual therapy.

HOW DO I FIND A GOOD GROUP THERAPIST?

It's important to consider the qualifications of a potential therapist. A professional group therapist has received special training in group therapy and meets certain professional criteria. That's where the American Group Psychotherapy Association can help. Clinical Members of the association have received special training in group therapy. In addition, a Certified Group Psychotherapist will have met strict professional criteria as well as ongoing continuing educational requirements.

When talking with therapists, here are four simple questions you may want to ask.

- What is your background?
- Given my specific situation, how do you think group would work for me?
- What are your credentials as a group therapist?
- Do you have special training that is relevant to my problem?

ABOUT THE AMERICAN GROUP PSYCHOTHERAPY ASSOCIATION

The American Group Psychotherapy Association is the oldest and largest professional association dedicated to the field of group psychotherapy. The association has more than 4,000 members and maintains the highest professional standards in the field. AGPA is a multi-disciplinary association, representing all of the group psychotherapy disciplines.

Group works! For information on finding a group psychotherapist, call 212-477-2677 or visit our website at www.groupsinc.org

American Group Psychotherapy Association
25 East 21st Street, 6th Floor
New York, New York10010
212-477-2677 telephone
212-979-6627 facsimile
www.groupsinc.org

This publication is supported by the Group Psychotherapy Foundation's Mitchell Hochberg Memorial Public Education Fund

CLIENT QUOTES

"When I went into group therapy, I was suffering from low-level depression. Through the group therapy experience, I remember feeling joy again."

"My work prompted me to go into group therapy. Suddenly, as a manager I was dealing with more people and needed to improve my interpersonal communications skills."

"Through group, I identified what I needed to work on as an individual and learned how to better deal with other people."

Glossary of Acronyms and Managed Care Terms*

Over the last few years, a host of new acronyms and expressions has invaded the lexicon of health care. Below are definitions for 20 terms used frequently in Psychotherapy Finances. Most relate to managed care, though many have broader applications as well.

ASO (administrative services only): An organization—often, an insurance company or MCO—contracting to provide billing, utilization review, claims processing, and other nonclinical services. In ASO contracts, the organization does not offer clinical services or take on financial risk for them.

Anchor Group (also known as a clinical group, core group, or key group): This is a provider group that arranges with a managed care organization to receive the lion's share of referrals within their area—usually for reduced rates. The group must be multidisciplinary, with the capability to take on a heavy administrative burden: case management, outcomes measurement, utilization review, and more.

AHP (accountable health plan): An organization that can act as both insurer and provider—delivering care *and* managing funds for the care.

Capitation: A payment plan where a managed care organization (MCO) or provider group takes an agreed upon dollar amount, and is then responsible for delivering whatever contracted services are needed during the contract period. The MCO or provider group is "at risk." They've taken the money and now they have to deliver the care.

Capitation Rate: In a capitated contract, you accept a per member, per month (PMPM) rate for providing contracted services. So, if the deal covers 10,000 lives and the PMPM rate is \$3, the contract pays \$360,000 per year (\$3 × 12 months × 10,000 lives).

Carve-Out: Separating a specific piece of a benefit program (i.e., behavioral health) for separate contracting. Managed care organizations that specialize in behavioral health are also known as behavioral health "carve-out" companies.

* Reprinted with permission from *Psychotherapy Finances* 24 6–7.

Case Rate: A fixed dollar amount, or lump sum, that you take when a patient is referred. That agreed upon amount covers the entire "episode of care," regardless of how much treatment is necessary. Again, you "take on risk" (provider assumes risk for treatment).

Direct Contracting: You contract directly with an employer to provide services to employees. No middleman, no managed care.

EDI (electronic data interchange, also known as electronic communication): The automated exchange of data (claims, clinical information, etc.) by computer. All the major MBHOs (see definition following) have EDI pilot programs under way, but the lack of industry-wide standards is an obstacle. Most billing software for therapists has electronic claims processing capability.

Gatekeeper: This is the person at the MCO who says yes or no. Nonemergency specialty services and hospital admissions must be preauthorized by the gatekeeper. (In many settings, this will be a primary care physician, but behavioral health providers often serve as gatekeepers for behavioral health services.)

HMO (health maintenance organization): A managed care organization (MCO) that delivers comprehensive medical services on a prepaid basis. The HMO receives a capitated payment from clients such as employers, government agencies, insurance companies, etc. in HMO plans, members must go through approved providers for services, and services generally must be preauthorized by a gatekeeper (preceding). Specialty services, such as mental health, may be carved out to an MBHO, large group practice, etc.

IDS (integrated delivery system): An arrangement between hospitals, physician groups, and other providers to be able to contract to provide comprehensive health care services. Some IDSs also offer their own health plan products and may be called accountable health plans (preceding) or "vertically integrated systems."

MBHO (managed behavioral health organization): A managed care company specializing in psychiatric or behavioral health services. MBHOs contract with a variety of clients, including HMOs, insurance companies, employers, government agencies, etc.

MCO (managed care organization): Companies that control the use of health care services, with the goal of providing appropriate services in a cost-effective manner. They do this by reviewing medical necessity, performing utilization review, incentivizing members to use certain providers, etc. MCOs often assume risk, taking capitated payments to manage care for a defined population. MCOs include HMOs, PPOs, POS plans, PHOs, IDS plans, and AHPs.

MSO (management services organization): These organizations may be owned by hospitals, large provider groups, MCOs, independent investors, etc. They contract with provider groups for management services such as billing, marketing, information systems, and more. Often, they receive a percentage of the group's revenue.

PCP (primary care physician or provider): The term "PCP" is applied to general practitioners, family doctors, general internists, and, at times, pediatricians and OB/GYNs. For MCOs, they coordinate care and often act as gatekeepers.

PPO (preferred provider organization): A network of hospitals, physicians, other providers, etc., which provides services to particular populations at discounted rates. The PPO may be a legal entity itself, contracting with insurers and other clients, or it may be part of an established health plan. PPOs are often used to provide some management of care in an indemnity (traditional insurance) setting. PPOs generally offer more choice and pay higher rates than HMO plans.

PSO (provider sponsored organization or provider services organization): A legal entity formed and majority-owned by affiliated providers to compete for managed care and other contracts. The PSO must meet federal and state requirements, and the providers must share substantial financial risk.

PHO (physician hospital organization): Generally, an organization created by a hospital and group of providers for the purpose of obtaining contracts. The PHO may own or subcontract with an MSO for management services. It may also own or subcontract with a health plan and other providers.

POS (point of service): A health plan that allows members to access care from nonparticipating or out-of-network providers for a higher copayment. Theoretically, this type of plan offers more choice of providers without severe penalties, but often the out-of-pocket expenses are substantially higher when a nonnetwork provider is used.

From *Psychotherapy Finances, 24, 9, 293*. September, 1998

Suggested Reading—
A Beginning

Bernard, H. S., & MacKenzie, K. R. (Eds.). (1994). *Basics of group psychotherapy.* New York: Guilford.

Fuhriman, A., & Burlingame, G. (Eds.). (1994). *Handbook of group psychotherapy: An empirical and clinical synthesis.* New York: John Wiley & Sons.

International Journal of Group Psychotherapy. (Subscription comes with American Group Psychotherapy Association membership.)

Kaplan, H. I., & Sadock, B. J. (Eds.). (1993). *Comprehensive group psychotherapy* (3rd ed.). Baltimore: Williams & Wilkins.

MacKenzie, K. R. (Ed.). (1995). *Effective use of group therapy in managed care.* Washington, DC: American Psychiatric Press.

MacKenzie, K. R., & Dies, R. R. (Eds.). (1983). *Advances in group psychotherapy.* American Group Psychotherapy Association, 1.

McKay, M., & Palea, K. (1992). *Focal group psychotherapy.* New York: Harbinger Publications, Inc.

Rutan, J. S., & Stone, W. N. (1984). *Psychodynamic group psychotherapy* (2nd ed.). New York: Macmillan.

Yalom, I. D. (1994). *The theory and practice of group psychotherapy* (4th ed.). New York: Basic Books.

INDEX